FREEMASONRY
and its Image of Man

J.G. Fichte, philosopher and mason,
wrote in 1800 his essay
Philosophy of Freemasonry. Today,
in ideal communion with Fichte, I too
present my Philosophy of Freemasonry,
which I dedicate to masons all over
the world.

GIULIANO DI BERNARDO

FREEMASONRY
and its Image of Man

A Philosophical Investigation

'Know then thyself, presume not God to scan,
The proper study of mankind is man.'

Alexander Pope

Giuliano di Bernardo

FREESTONE

1989

British Library Cataloguing in Publication Data

Di Bernardo, Giuliano
Freemasonry and its image of man: a philosophical investigation
1. Freemasonry
I. Title
366′.1

ISBN 0-7104-5001-X

First published in Italian by Marsilio Editore, Venice

First English edition published by Freestone, an imprint of Weald UK Ltd

Translated by Guy Aston and Giuliano di Bernardo

 Enquiries to:
D J Costello (Publishers) Ltd
43 The High Street
Tunbridge Wells
Kent
TN1 1XL

Typeset in 11 on 13 pt Century by
Staples Printers (Rochester) Limited

Printed by Billing and Sons Ltd, Worcester

Contents

Preface

Guiliano di Bernardo was initiated into Freemasonry in 1961 and is well known in Italian and International Masonic Circles. He is as well internationally renowned in the field of social sciences and is an acknowledged scholar of the Philosophy of Science. In addition he is the author of a number of books which have been published in several languages.

This book 'Freemasonry and Its Image of Man', is the first, extensively revised, English language edition of the author's *Filosofia della Massoneria* originally published in Italy in 1987 and a German language version of this edition is also currently in preparation. It is intended by the author to be essentially a philosophical approach to Freemasonry and to its anthropological aspects and it makes a careful examination of the concept of Freemasonry within the context and significance of masonic symbols.

Although a great deal of what is contained in the book might be considered as an academic treatise, reviewing various theories put forward by the author, he presents these in the context of a purposeful approach to the many questions of common interest which the subject of Freemasonry inevitably brings up.

Ample discussion is given, for example, to the delicate questions revolving around Freemasonry and Religion, and Freemasonry and the Roman Catholic Church and Freemasonry and the State.

Freemasonry has from time to time been accused of being incompatible with religion. The historical reasons for this, for the negative attitude of the Roman Catholic Church towards Freemasonry and the ambiguous statements of present day thinking are discussed at length. Applying the methods of Philosophical study to this question, the author endorses the declaration issued by the United Grand Lodge of England concerning Freemasonry and Religion, and expresses his own ideas on how the subject might be conceived and interpreted from a Philosophical point of view.

The role of Freemasonry in society and its relationship with the State is another matter of considerable historical significance. Progressive ideals and the principles of Freedom, Tolerance and Justice have always characterised Freemasonry and have directly helped to influence the development of democratic societies. The author reviews the evolution of historical events in the world which resulted from this and the difficulties sometimes encountered from forces opposed to such ideals.

Although the theories expressed and the arguments presented in this book are naturally those of the author, and do not represent any form of official statement, I feel sure that this work will make an important contribution to masonic thought and debate and be received with interest, stimulating all who read it, as it has done for me, to make their own judgements and formulate their own ideas and opinions.

Leslie H. Hicks
February 1989

Introduction

Philosophical reflection has traditionally concerned itself with metaphysics, the theory of knowledge, logic, ethics and aesthetics. It has also considered specific disciplines such as science, history, law, politics and religion and, as a consequence, the philosophy of science, history, law, politics and religion. When mankind became an object of its investigation, there naturally followed philosophical anthropology, or the conception of man from a philosophical point of view.

The anthropologies proposed by schools of philosophy and individual thinkers are varied and can be classified according to different criteria. For our current purposes we need only explain two:

1 that which divides anthropologies into *religious* and *lay*
2 that which classifies them as *exclusivist* and *non-exclusivist.*

An anthropology is *religious* if man is considered in terms of his relationship with God, his claimed creator, while it is *lay* if the nature of man is defined separately from this relationship with the divine.

An anthropology is *exclusivist* if it is based on certain specific values, whilst it is *non-exclusivist* if it is founded on common values belonging both to its own specific anthropology and also to others.

Religious anthropology is by its very nature exclusivist, since the values accepted are only those which constitute the specific contents of that religion. It follows then that there can be no compatibility between a religious anthropology (characterised by a grouping together of specific values) and any other (characterised by other specific values). In a certain sense, one can accept pluralism but only within the context of the various attitudes that can be assumed within the same religious anthropology, where the possibility of supporting theses which in some respects may differ in relation to each other, can be accepted.

On the other hand, lay anthropology is by its very nature, non-exclusivist and therefore pluralist, since it is founded on values that are common to various anthropologies. In this case, the values that are shared are those very common ones, while the specific values of the single anthropologies are either set aside or they lose their specific meaning.

The anthropology which characterises Freemasonry is lay and non-exclusivist. It is lay because it does not *demand* a belief in the creation of Man by the God of any specific religion, though as I will show in chapter 6, individual masons may hold this belief. It is non-exclusivist in the sense that, by aiming to attain a universal harmony among all men, it takes only common values as its characteristic features.

Freemasonry is not an all-inclusive philosophy. It does not pretend to find answers to questions regarding all the areas with which philosophy has traditionally been concerned. What Freemasonry does is to provide a precise, practical philosophy regarding man, his nature and his aims—a determinate anthropology that attempts to define the constituent elements of the Freemason.

Lay and non-exclusivist masonic anthropology has another characteristic. In fact by delineating its own image of man, Freemasonry has purposely renounced any investigation into all man's possible aspects, and takes into consideration only those concerning his ethical self-improvement. This does not mean that these other aspects have no value for masonic thought, but rather that they are secondary and subordinate to ethical values. Indeed, it is because Freemasonry emphasises the study of a particular aspect of man (his moral aspect) that its anthropology is, by definition, partial. This is one of the most important differences between Freemasonry and religion. While every anthropology originating from religion is by nature *total*, masonic anthropology is *partial*.

Can it become total? As I will try to show in Chapter 6, the answer is yes: not as far as Freemasonry as such is concerned, but certainly with regard to the individual mason to whom the right to integrate his personal partial anthropology with elements belonging to other anthropologies is recognised. Therefore, masonic anthropology appears to be a non-exclusivist anthropology, a matrix of different anthropologies which nevertheless all converge towards the same moral image of man. And it is here that an important distinction is highlighted within Freemasonry considered as a society of men. On the one hand, there are masons who feel they are realised in partial anthropology, while on the other, there are those who feel the need to give it a deeper sense, and therefore aspire towards a total anthropology. In chapter 6, I shall refer to the first type of mason as "regulativist" and the second type as "religious".

By confining masonic anthropology as such to simple ethical self-improvement, one may reach the conclusion that masonic thought is *immanentistic*—that is concerned only with the here and now—and materialistic. This is not true, since Freemasonry does not reduce everything to ethics, but also takes into account other aspects that characterise mankind.

It is from a desire to avoid this type of misunderstanding that the idea of *transcendence* is introduced, represented in Freemasonry by the Great Architect of the Universe, whose precise role it is to ensure objectivity in subjectively shared values, and from whom the same idea of the ethical self-improvement of man derives (on this point see Chapters 2 and 6).

The pursuit of ethical goals occurs according to initiatic modalities, that is on the basis of rituals and symbols which confer on Freemasonry the typical characteristics of an initiatic society.

Our considerations so far have afforded a definition of Freemasonry as a conception of man requiring the pursuit of ethical aims directed by transcendence according to initiation. This is the philosophical expression of the standard definition of Freemasonry as 'a peculiar system of morality, veiled in allegory and illustrated by symbols'.

A specific element in the masonic conception of man, which derives from its characteristic of non-exclusivity, is its tendency to universality. This feature is not to be found in any other conception of man. So for example, every religious anthropology, which by definition is total, aspires to the uniting of all men but only if they declare themselves ideally committed to it. The society of Christians consists only of those who profess the Christian faith. The same goes for other religions, and generally speaking, for all other conceptions of man. On the other hand, Freemasonry proposes that men sharing total and different anthropologies should join together in a society, thus realising universality and at the same time avoiding conflict between its initiates. How is this possible? In my opinion, the solution is to be found in the philosophical thesis that I have called *non-exclusive regulativism,* on the basis of which the society of masons consists of men who have partial anthropology in common (represented by the ethical foundation) which can however be integrated with other anthropologies (not just religious ones). From this it follows that masons cannot cause conflict amongst themselves from their individually shared anthropologies.

The concept of universality must not be confused with that of totality. Whilst the latter refers to the conception of man (which may be partial or total), the former concerns an effective modality of association between men, each of whom can share a total anthropology. We can even say that the concept of universality characterises Freemasonry understood as a society of men (I will show in Chapter 6 that Freemasonry may also be understood as a concept).

If Freemasonry is characterised by the pursuit of ethical aims within an anthropological framework oriented towards universality, its main task cannot be reached without a deeper knowledge of man with respect to his different and concrete manifestations. This knowledge, however, is not simply limited to describing man as he is in reality, but it considers him as he *ought-to-be* with regard to the aims he should pursue, which represent the ideal point of reference of ethical self-improvement. To realise this, Freemasonry proposes a global project characterised by its own anthropology. Nevertheless, if masonic anthropology expresses that which is unchangeable, the project of man's self-improvement will always be historically conditioned. It follows that masonic anthropology (a constant foundation of masonic thought) finds different realisations in different historical periods. This is where the relationship between the ideal and philosophical plane (characterised mainly by the conception of man) and the concrete and historical plane (characterised by its numerous manifestations) is captured. Authentic comprehension can only be attained if the philosophical and historical planes are explained in terms of their reciprocal relationship.

Freemasonry therefore has the task of relating its own conception of man to various manifestations of history, past and present. Historically Freemasonry has played an active role in human events, but the questions are now being raised—What is the task of Freemasonry in the world in which we live? and—Is its existence still justifiable? Anyone asking the latter question is not aware of the true nature of Freemasonry, which is initiatic, and therefore not confined to any one historical period. This misunderstanding may derive from the fact that Freemasonry is interpreted in a limited sense with respect to its political and social achievements. For example, one could assert that as American masons, inspired by the principles of Freemasonry, fought for and actually achieved the independence of their country there is no longer any reason for Freemasonry to exist in America. But for Freemasonry, understood as an initiatic society, there may or may not be any political or social engagement, and this in any event takes second place to the true aims that it pursues. In brief, the initiatic nature of Freemasonry will never end as long as there is a man who shares the masonic anthropology.

The question 'What is the task of Freemasonry in the world in which we live?' implies a knowledge of this world in all its most significant aspects—scientific, technological, economic, political, social, religious and spiritual. It is only from such a knowledge that Freemasonry can draw up and propose a global project for the betterment of mankind. Man and society, under the specific pressure of science, are rapidly changing. But not all changes are for the better. We have only to think of certain recent developments in the biological sciences which seem to be directed beyond the limits imposed by a respect for human nature (see Chapter 7). Freemasonry must exercise its moral authority and guard carefully against such deviations. But to exercise such authority, it must be clear about its model for the betterment of mankind which can come only from its own anthropology. Only in this way will Freemasonry be able to carry out its true function—the material, moral and spiritual improvement of man.

Chapter 1

The Modern Origins of Freemasonry

The term 'Freemasonry' or 'Free Masonry' originates from the French and is derived from 'Maszun', 'Massoune mestre'. It was brought to England by the Normans and transformed into 'Freemason'. The term 'Mason' without the prefix 'free' appeared as far back as 1292 in a document on the construction of a chapel in the Palace of Westminster and the expression 'Freemasonry' first appeared in 1375 in a note regarding a meeting of representatives of the City Corporations in London. The same expression is found in 1396 in a list of workers building Exeter Cathedral. These numerous variations of 'Freemasonry' show that there are still some doubts as to where the term originated.

As far as the origins of Freemasonry itself are concerned, we must distinguish between history and legend. Its legendary or mythical origins are mentioned in the 1723 Constitutions of Anderson, where Freemasonry begins with Adam, created in the image of the Great Architect of the Universe. Adam taught his children Freemasonry. Cain constructed a city which he dedicated to Enoch his first son, and Noah, ninth descendent of Seth, constructed the Ark according to the rules of Freemasonry. After the Flood Noah and his three sons handed down the traditions and arts of Freemasonry to their descendents. This art spread throughout Greece and Sicily and reached its peak in the Roman Empire. All trace of it was lost in Brittany after the

Romans, but thanks to Carlo Martello, England recovered the tradition of Masonic Art after the Saxon invasions. Anderson took his version of the history of Freemasonry up to 1723.

These legends are to be interpreted according to their symbolic and esoteric significance. They express the conviction that Freemasonry has existed since the beginning of mankind because it reflects a deep need of the human mind. Freemasonry was created at the same time as man and has evolved alongside him. Just as man possesses a sense of religiosity and sacredness, likewise he has an inherent sense of masonic ethical universality. Freemasonry therefore particularly reflects an unsuppressible dimension of man: an ethical dimension, oriented by transcendence, expressed by initiatiory modalities.

One cannot characterise the modern origins of Freemasonry without explaining its development from an operative to a speculative form. However Freemasonry has never been purely operative, that is solely dedicated to material construction. It has always pursued speculative ends to some extent as a result of the religious principles it shares. How and why then did this transformation of artisan and operative Freemasonry into a spiritual and speculative form come about, especially since the latter, without losing the symbolic tradition, has become the expression of a universal activity for the construction of an ideal Temple? The first reason was the decline of its operative foundations. As far back as the fifteenth century the corporations of builders, whose work consisted mainly of the construction of cathedrals, were in a state of crisis. They started to break up halfway through the sixteenth century. The second reason involved the presence in the corporations of the 'accepted' members. This was an age-old custom. The clergy and nobility, representatives of different power groups, both fundamental to the existence of the corporations, had always been accepted. But as the state of crisis in the operative element deepened the number of the 'accepted' increased to such an extent that they became far more numerous than the workers themselves. Gradually, operative activity took second place, with the symbolic work of the construction of a spiritual and invisible Temple becoming the main aim of the 'new' Freemasonry.

The transformation from operative to speculative occured in English Lodges, since it was only in England that traditional, operative Freemasonry was still alive, though in decline. In Germany and France on the other hand the united brotherhoods of Free Masons were accused of spreading social and religious disorder. They were forced to limit their activities to charitable works. Thus the conditions necessary for the birth of modern Freemasonry existed only in England.

The rise of speculative Freemasonry brought with it the danger of alienating the age-old authentic tradition of free masons. In fact the opening of the Temples to the 'accepted' and to their cultural, religious, political and social ideas gave, on one hand, the undoubted advantage of universalising a field which until then had been restricted to the demands of the master craftsmen. On the other hand it laid itself open to the risk of conflicts emerging between supporters of different tendencies. This was how the idea of creating a supreme masonic body whose main task was to judge the regularity of the Lodges originated on 24th June 1717, St John's Day, when four Lodges in London, *The Goose and Gridiron, The Crown, The Apple Tree and The Rummer and Grapes*, decided to join together in a Grand Lodge. A few years later, on the basis of these simple origins, an idealistic movement developed and spread throughout the world. Let us follow the preliminary stages of this movement in Europe and the United States, giving special mention to particularly significant cases but not in any specific order.

Within Europe Britain was in a privileged position. Not all the Lodges joined the newly formed Grand Lodge of London in 1717. A number of masons remained tied to the operative tradition since they considered too revolutionary, in respect of their Christian beliefs, the acceptance of deism as the foundation of a natural religion in which 'all men agree'. Consequently an invitation to tolerance was understood as a denial of the highest masonic principles. Furthermore the Lodges of the counties were not willing to give up their autonomy. The Lodge of York thus became the point of reference for all those opposing the Grand Lodge and in 1725 became known as The Grand Lodge of All England. Thus a schism occurred in English Freemasonry. On one side there was the Grand Lodge of London which welcomed the masons called *Moderns*, while on the other there was The Grand Lodge of the Free and Accepted Masons According to the Old Institutions whose members were called *Antients*. In spite of the inevitable controversies the prestige of English Freemasonry became so great that men of all social ranks aspired to membership. Members of the Royal Family were initiated and held positions of high office within the two Grand Lodges. Conflict eased but it was not until 1813 that the two Grand Lodges were reconciled. On the basis of an agreement called *The Articles of Union*, The United Grand Lodge of Ancient Freemasons of England came into being. The causes of the split between English masons were wisely removed or minimised. For example, the deistic religion of Anderson was replaced by a form of personal theism. Furthermore, whilst the spirit of tradition was preserved, the principle of tolerance was accepted as an innovatory element, having been imposed by the new liberal demands of English society, on the basis of which the god of masons was no longer exlusively the Christian God. The United

Grand Lodge of England was recognised as *The Grand Mother Lodge of The World.*

In some respects Freemasonry in France developed differently. First there was the claim of its modern origins. In 1777 the Grand Orient of France decreed that its Constitution, derived from the Lodge of the regiment of the Royal Irish Guards, dated back to 1688. In that year Freemasonry appeared in France with the arrival of the Stuarts and their Scottish and Irish regiments. Thus Freemasonry in France predated the creation of the Grand Lodge of London in 1717.

Freemasonry spread rapidly in France. First because it devised a way of getting round the problem of admitting women (there were many high ranking women in this period who played an important part in affirming Masonic ideas). Second because Papal Bulls of Excommunication were not applied (the French Parliament was supposed to have ratified them but chose not to).

In 1738 an assembly of all the 'English' and 'Scottish' Lodges formed *La Grande Loge de France* and nominated Louis de Pardoillan de Gondrin, Duke of Antin, Grand Master. On his death jealousies and conflicts arose compromising the stability of Freemasonry. *Le Grand Orient de France* was created in 1773 imposing formal statutes and regulating relations between the Lodges in an attempt to overcome this critical situation. However not all masons accepted the decisions of the new Grand Orient and many remained faithful to the Grand Lodge of France. The two allegiances continued until the Revolution.

The Grand Orient laid down foundations for French Freemasonry that were infused with ideals of liberty and equality. The Lodge *Les Neuf Soeurs* was set up and became the meeting point of the leading spirits of enlightened thought of the period: Montesquieu, Diderot, Helvetius, Lalande, Condorcet, Lacépède, Marquis Lafayette, d'Alembert, André Chenier, Abbé Sieyès, Camille Desmoulins, Danton and many others came together under its auspices. Other Lodges too initiated great thinkers such as Mirabeau, Beauharnais, Beaumarchais, Joseph de Maistre, Baron Holbach, Massena and Talleyrand. Voltaire was initiated at the age of 84 into the *Les Neuf Soeurs*, in the presence of 250 Brothers.

Thus Freemasonry came to be the highest expression of the ideal and cultural movements of the Eighteenth Century and spread among the most authoritative exponents of the bourgeoisie, clergy, nobility, law, army and culture.

In 1789 the outbreak of the Revolution marked different destinies for French masons. Some of them, such as Talleyrand, Lafayette, Danton, Sieyès, Chamfort, Candorcet and Marat were active revolutionaries. Others like Calonne, Montmorency and Demoulins, supported the idea of change but were antagonistic to the excesses of 'the Terror', and either resisted or emigrated. The guillotine made no distinction between royalists and revolutionaries.

A significant event in the development of French Freemasonry was the abolition in 1877 of the formula of The Great Architect of the Universe which was a move to express as clearly as possible the principle of freedom of conscience. In this way French masons withdrew from having to commit themselves on the nature of The Great Architect. This decision was destined to cause great dissension with other allegiances in the world. English masons immediately broke off relations with the Grand Orient of France, not only because they saw in the abolition of the formula of The Great Architect of the Universe the possibility of accepting atheism and materialism into the Lodges, but also (and most critically) because it was a departure from the habits and customs of Ancient and Modern Freemasonry in which The Great Architect of the Universe was a common feature.

The first modern Lodges in Germany were also of English origin. The first German Lodge was founded in Hamburg in 1737 and took the name of Absalon some years later. This Lodge had the honour of initiating on 4th August 1738, the Prince Royal of Prussia—the future Frederick II—who did a great deal for the prestige of Freemasonry in Europe. A myriad of Grand Lodges came into being when, in the eighteenth century, the German States were divided. Consequently, the history of German Freemasonry can be identified with the history of these Grand Lodges, which were:

The Grand Mother Lodge of the Three Globes, Berlin
The Grand Lodge of Prussia
The National Grand Lodge of German Freemasons, Berlin
The Grand Lodge of Hamburg
The Grand Lodge of the Sun, Bayreuth
The Grand Mother Lodge of the Eclectic Union, Frankfurt
The National Grand Lodge of Saxony, Dresden
The Grand Lodge Concord, Darmstadt
The Grand Lodge Chain of German Brotherhood, Leipzig
The Grand Lodge Freimaurerbund, Nuremburg
The Symbolic Grand Lodge, Hamburg (later Berlin)

In spite of the proliferation of Grand Lodges, German Freemasonry had some typically Teutonic features. The romantic spirit and interest in the transcendent, always a feature of German culture, found fertile ground in the initiatic and esoteric tradition of Freemasonry. The Temple became the meeting-place for scholars of alchemy, magic, hermetic art, theurgy and sorcery. Forms of mysticism were prevalent. Thoughts flew to the ineffable and mysterious. The more esoteric aspects of man came to be reconsidered in a universal and cosmopolitan perspective, following the reactions of French and English Illuminism. German Freemasonry aspired to its own philosophy reflected in the works of some of its most illustrious followers—Lessing, Wieland, Herder, Goethe, Fichte, Werner, Mozart and Haydn.

The movement of the *Illuminati of Bavaria*, a mutual aid association with social and scientific educational aims played an important part in the development of German Freemasonry. Although they had nothing to do with Freemasonry, they made their way into the Lodges and took possession of initiatic work, creating considerable havoc and confusion. Accused of plotting against the State and Church, the Illuminati and masons with them, found themselves subject to persecution. In 1784, the Duke Elector of Bavaria issued a decree against all Brotherhoods that had arisen without the sovreign's approval. The movement of the Illuminati was seriously hit by this and other decrees and were soon eliminated. It had completely disappeared by the start of the French Revolution.

English masons were also responsible for the foundation of the first Lodge in Italy. This took place in Florence around 1730. Italian Freemasonry subsequently spread throughout the peninsula to Rome, Naples, Padua, Venice, Modena, Livorno and Lucca and other important cities. Fortunatly it did not have to face any major opposition at its inception or during its early development. Indeed it quickly found its place in the initiatic tradition that had been kept alive throughout the previous centuries and was able to add its own contribution. The first trauma that beset it was the Bull of Excommunication in 1738 of Pope Clement XII, who accused masons of plotting against religion and forbade Catholics from entering Masonic Lodges. This was the first act of a drama that was to continue for centuries to come and which still seriously jeopardises the relationship between Freemasonry and the Catholic Church.

Towards the end of the eighteenth century, the picture in Italy changed: there were Lodges connected with Grand Lodge of London, others with the Grand Orient of Holland and the Scottish Mother Lodge of Marseilles, others influenced by German Freemasonry and the Illuminati of Bavaria. Thia state of confusion continued until the nineteenth century, when Garibaldi, with the support of Cavour and Mazzini was instrumental in bringing together many of the diverse Lodges and Grand Lodges, under the jurisdiction of the Grand Orient of Italy.

In the eighteenth century, Freemasonry spread rapidly in Central Europe through the Balkans, Switzerland, Belgium, the Netherlands and Luxemburg, and throughout Sweden, Denmark, Norway, Iceland, Russia, Poland, Finland, Spain and Portugal.

There was already a Provincial Grand Master in 1730 in the English colonies in America and the first Lodge was formed in Philadelphia in 1731. Benjamin Franklin—who American masons have to thank for the first published edition of Anderson's Constitutions—was initiated into this Lodge. In later years he became its Worshipful Master. George Washington was initiated in the Fredericksburg Lodge in Virginia on 4th November 1752 and Lodges were formed in all of the American colonies.

At the beginning of the American Revolution, Freemasonry was the only idealistic tie uniting men from different national and religious backgrounds. This helps to explain why masons played such a major role in the revolt against England. Freemasonry reflected an ideal. In Boston, a culturally rich and open city, the St Andrew's Lodge became the centre of the rebellion. The authors of the Revolution for the freedom of the American people were nearly all masons. Among them were Washington, Franklin, Otis, Adams, Hamilton, Henry, Marshall, Madison and Allen, Baron Steufen from Germany and Lafayette from France. Fifty out of the fifty-six men who signed the Declaration of Independence were masons. However not all masons supported Washington and many continued to be loyal to the British Crown.

The American Revolution benefitted from the contribution, both moral and material, of some important Europeans. However, the liberal conception of 'the State' set forth in the Declaration of Independence was transferred to Europe and to France in particular. Franklin, the highly respected ambassador of the United States of Northern America to Paris, became the Worshipful Master of the Parisian Lodge *Les Neuf Soeurs* and propogated the ideals of humanity that the American Brothers had proclaimed in the Revolution, and as a result Freemasonry spread throughout the rest of the world.

Chapter 2

The Masonic Conception Of Man

In this chapter my intentions are to examine the notions that are needed to clarify the definition of Freemasonry as a conception of man requiring the pursuit of ethical aims directed by *transcendence* according to initiatic modalities.

First, the concepts of Freemasonry can be divided into *initiatic* and *profane*. Those concepts whose meaning is known only to masons are called initiatic, while those comprehensible to all are profane.

The fundamental initiatic concept is 'the secret'. Fundamental profane concepts are 'freedom', 'tolerance', 'brotherhood', 'transcendence'. From these fundamental concepts stem others both initiatic and profane, such as 'equality', 'love', 'kindness', 'charity', 'respect', 'solidarity' and 'self-improvement'.

We must analyse what the four fundamental profane concepts signify. Let us begin with the concept of freedom.

Before going on to examine some of its basic meanings we should first emphasise that freedom is an insuppressible and irrefutable datum in our life experience. We know we are free when we find ourselves having to choose between two or more alternatives in a personal and responsible way. The experience of freedom is mainly expounded in moral decision That is in decisions for or against a moral value. This is where, as we shall see later, the freedom of man acquires its most authentic meaning. Whereas we may deny freedom in theory, in real life we can only act in its presupposition. Freedom is also presupposed in social life where concepts such as good and evil, justice and injustice, punishment and reward, would have no sense if they did not have at their roots an experience of freedom. Therefore we always presuppose our own freedom and that of others in our choices and actions.

Given that freedom is an irrefutable experience in man's life, I will go on to examine some of its basic meanings.

According to one definition of freedom, man is free if, and only if, he is really able to adhere to an objective order of values and if he is capable of sharing it subjectively. This means that man experiences in the society in which he lives, a set of values that are objective since they already existed before he came into being, and also because they can be shared by other men. However in order to be able to act, man has to accept and thus choose certain values. This acceptance involves making subjective values considered in an objective sense in a given society.

This definition of freedom is a constituent part of man, in the sense that man is man if, and only if, he is free. If man were not free, then he would not be man. When we speak of freedom we are referring not only to material freedom but to all possible and imaginable forms. This is essential if we wish to understand the constitutive nature of freedom. We may chain a man to a rock and deprive him of all his material freedom, yet we cannot forbid him to think of freedom, to conceive worlds in which he feels free. Only if we were able to take away from him his capacity to think of freedom would we be depriving him of the very nature of man: indeed, he would no longer be a man.

This definition of freedom does not refer to man's capacity of choice, and so does not take his responsibility into account. Therefore, we must integrate the above with the notion of freedom as a capacity of choice. This notion is derived from the presupposition that man is, in some way or other, responsible for the choices he makes, in view of a reward or punishment. If he makes a responsible choice of a subjective order that does not correspond to an objective one, then he is liable to be punished; if, on the other hand, he sticks to an objective order even in particularly difficult circumstances, then he deserves to be rewarded. Therefore we must add to the above definition of freedom the following condition: man is free if, and only if, he can make a responsible choice between various alternatives.

In order to better illustrate this definition of freedom let me give some examples from the history of philosophical thought.

We will begin with a concept of freedom that has been at the heart of European individualistic and liberalist tradition. According to this freedom refers mainly to conditions characterised by the absence of coercion by the State or any other authority. This concept of freedom, which is mostly clearly formulated by John Stuart Mill in his essay *On Liberty*, has been developed more fully elsewhere. In fact some scholars maintain that this idea of freedom must be taken further, that is, the conditions necessary for freedom to exist should be

1 the absence of coercion on the part of man
2 the absence of natural impediments
3 the possession of a means and power to reach the objectives which man chooses on the basis of his own volition.

The concept of coercion at the base of this conception of freedom requires further clarification. Let us consider, for example, the following declaration of Bertrand Russell:

> *Generally speaking, freedom can be defined as the absence of obstacles in the realisation of one's desires.*

Such a vague formulation lays the way open to more than one possible interpretation. For example, let us imagine that in a given society, governors and educators have been so successful in manipulating and controlling the consciences of all their citizens that the citizens therefore desire all that the governors wish them to, without supposing there may be any alternatives to the object of their desire.

This is an extreme case and an ideal one which however demonstrates how in all societies consciences are manipulated to a greater or lesser extent. It indicates basically that the desires of the citizens are exactly the same as those of the governors. In this kind of society man may feel free, but is he? If we can say of this scenario that coercion does not exist, then there must be freedom.

Yet for freedom to exist, we should explain what this requirement is that calls for a knowledge of alternatives. If by freedom we mean man's right to choose between various alternatives, then this right in itself implies that the alternatives must be known to those who choose. There is freedom if, and only if, man makes a responsible and conscious choice in favour of one of the various alternatives that he has before him.

The sense of freedom that we have considered so far can be understood as 'freedom from' (for example, coercion). There is, however, another sense of freedom that can be interpreted as 'freedom of'. In the political and social field in particular, requests are made to obtain certain types of freedom. Thus, an abstract class with various kinds of freedom is formed: freedom of thought, speech, association, meeting, work, movement and so on. Absence of coercion is understood here too, and consequently, the capacity of man to choose and act responsibly on the basis of his own will. It is clear that requests to obtain the above forms of freedom, even if in reference to an abstract class of general kinds of freedom, are still conditioned by particular cases in which general kinds of freedom find concrete realisation.

This analysis of this notion of freedom makes no reference to the objective order expressing the possibility man has of adhering subjectively to an objective order of values.

We must insist on this latter component of the concept of freedom because without it, all other notions of freedom would be devoid of meaning. What is the point of freedom 'from' and freedom 'of' if they cannot be directed towards an objective scale of values, capable of justifying the exercising of freedom itself? In particular, freedom, understood as a capacity to adhere to an objective order of values, is an essential presupposition for a moral dimension to be set up in man.

We can now consider one of the more important aspects of freedom, that is, its relation to moral issues. Freedom is the first basic condition of morality. Morality is possible only on the basis of freedom: without freedom, there is no morality. Whenever freedom is denied, there is no room left for a true understanding of morality.

This justifies the choice, on the part of masonic thinking, of freedom as a fundamental concept. In fact, Freemasonry conceives a subjectively shared moral order as the highest realisation of initiatic perfection. Therefore, since freedom is the primary source of the ethical life of man and the generating element of the ethical dimension, it is only natural that it should be taken to be a primary concept in the masonic conception of man.

The principle of tolerance is closely connected to the theme of freedom. Among its supporters are Bodin *(République)*, Montaigne *(De la Liberté de Conscience)*, Spinoza *(Tractatus Theologico-Politicus)*, Locke *(Epistola de Tolerantia)*, John Stuart Mill *(On Liberty)*.

The first systematic argument in favour of tolerance comes from Locke, who maintained that the repression and use of force cannot make a man accept a faith or belief into the depths of his soul. At most, they can make him become an orthodox believer. This policy is not only useless, but also morally wrong, since it provokes hypocrisy. This is why Locke refutes the Catholic theory according to which strength may be a necessary instrument for bringing man to salvation. He also rejects the theory according to which the duties of man towards the Church are the same as his duties towards the State, since civilised society would fall into a state of anarchy if religious dissent were tolerated. Locke, in fact, describes the Church as a 'voluntary society' whose mission in the world is independent from the functions of the State. Indeed, the Church exists in order to save man's soul, and this aim can be reached only through persuasion and non-violent means. On the other hand, the State exists in order to protect human rights, for which reason the use of force, as an extreme sanction, is a necessary condition in the exercising of its functions. It is not the responsibility of the State to save the soul, just as it is not the task of the Church to use force. The State has no knowledge of what true religion is, and so it cannot impose any. It is in every man's right to have his own faith, and he must be respected in this.

Locke's argument in favour of tolerance is taken up again by John Stuart Mill who generally agrees but poses some minor limitations to its validity. Whereas Locke urges that man's freedom be protected from State and Church interference, Mill demands that the principle of tolerance be extended from the political to the moral sphere.

Now we can formulate two fundamental meanings of the concept of tolerance.

> 1 Tolerance is an attitude which in principle refutes a way of thinking that is considered wrong, yet tolerates it out of a feeling of respect for the freedom of others. This leaves room for a way of thought of one's own.
>
> 2 Tolerance is an attitude of indifference with respect to any way of thinking, in which no opinion is shared, but in which one is committed only to a liberal attitude. In this case, there is no room for a way of thought of one's own.

Freemasonry adheres only to the former of these two definitions. It recognises the existence of ways of thought other than its own, and nonetheless maintains that other ways of thought should be allowed to exist. Freemasonry cannot accept the latter definition: it is neither agnostic nor indifferent to the ways of thought of others.

Freemasonry is neither everything nor the opposite of everything. Yet it does possess its own precise philosophy which, as we shall see later, gives rise to a clear philosophical anthropology, that is, a given conception of man, which while not refuting the contribution of other anthropologies, is placed at the roots of its vision of the world.

The third profane fundamental concept characteristic of Freemasonry is that of Brotherhood. The idea of Brotherhood dates back to the remotest times in the history of mankind. It can be supposed that the bond that first tied one man to another was that of blood and that subsequently this was extended to the tribe or community. It reappears with the Christian message. All men are commonly dependent on the creative act of God: all men therefore are sons of God and as such, brothers. In modern times this concept characterises the intuition of society as a cosmopolitan organism and becomes part of the values exalted by Illuminism.

As far as the lay conception of life is concerned, one's relationship to The Father is characterised in a very specific way: The Father is no longer God, but a unity of shared moral principles. In any case Brotherhood is nothing other than an attitude in which man maintains that other men are his specular image and that he shares the same rights with them. In this way then, we can establish that in man's relationship to his fellow beings, there is no difference between them as far as enjoying rights is concerned. Contrary to the concept of equality, Brotherhood allows one to capture the differences existing between men, as well as what they have basically in common. Men are equal in respect to their rights, but different in respect to their subjective characteristics (of intelligence, sensitivity, etc.) with which they face the problems of life and society. This is why I have placed Brotherhood, and not equality, among the fundamental concepts.

Brotherhood is closely related to tolerance: when I concede the possibility of other men professing ideas different to mine, I show that I am predisposed towards them in such a way as to consider them just as worthy as I am, and as such they are my brothers. As we shall see more clearly later, this is a crucial concept in the *immanent* (ie here and now) life of man. But can man acquire a deeper sense of his perfection by remaining within the limits of immanence? And in particular, can a mason progress with the smoothing of his rough stone if he excludes a transcendent principle? The answer is decidedly no. The reasons for such a decisive answer bring us to the fourth profane fundamental concept of Freemasonry—that of *transcendence.*

The concept of transcendence assumes two profoundly different meanings: a) transcendence understood ontologically, and b) transcendence as a regulative ideal.

When speaking of transcendence we are alluding to a foundation of reality that transcends, or goes beyond the limited horizon of that which we can experience. In this way the concept of transcendence opposes the alternative concept of immanence, present in every philosophical conception, which encloses the foundation of things in the totality of our experience. However, transcendence can be conceived in two different ways—ontological or regulative. Transcendence is understood in the former sense if the foundation transcending the horizon of experience is conceived as something that is *real in itself*: that is something that really does exist, even if it lies beyond our capacity of experience.

On the other hand, transcendence is understood in the regulative sense if, albeit not recognising any real existence in the foundation of things, it serves to make us consider the world from a Kantian point of view, *as if* it depended upon (and therefore was guaranteed as) on their being a respective transcendent foundation. To share, then, a regulative idea of transcendence is not the same as maintaining that the transcendent is real but, in spite of this, it means laying down the premises for us to behave ethically as if it actually existed.

For a clearer understanding of this distinction, let us examine it in the light of Christian and masonic conceptions of man.

According to Christian anthropology, man lives in a state of need on account of his being unable to attain certain fundamental aspirations. Man's sense of life derives from an horizon of definitive validity of his free activity. A Christian believes that there is a corresponding objective sense to such definitiveness, and that in the objective sense there is also a corresponding ontological way of comprehending the transcendent.

In fact, the Christian maintains that he can achieve full realisation in the transcendent and bring together into one whole all his component parts. Therefore, in the Christian conception, the transcendent has an ontological valence: it represents a world that is truly reachable to man.

This is made possible not so much by the possibilities man is capable of, as by the specific redemptive intervention of Christ. Reaching the transcendent is an actual possibility granted to man.

Even in the masonic way of thinking, man finds himself in a state of need, yet a mason does not believe in the demand for definitiveness nor in the corresponding objective sense. For a mason, the state of need is related to a transcendent with a regulative valence. Therefore he does not attribute an ontological valence to the transcendent, which one would have if man were granted a real possibility of attaining it. Vice versa, he understands it only as an unattainable goal, towards which he must make his pledge to improve himself by gradual approximation. The regulative ideal, which is based on the intrinsic conditions in man and not in the intervention of the transcendent, is given by a unity of contents which should be realised in the immanent: the transcendent orientates the immanent without being reduced to it.

Another difference between masonic anthropology and Christian anthropology (generally speaking, all anthropology that derives from a religion) concerns the notion of truth.

For the Christian, truth is absolute, eternal and immutable. It is revealed directly from God. Man can do nothing but accept it and take it up as a general principle that directs his actions in the world. Acceptance of truth means adhering to a religious vision of the world based on dogma.

For the mason, on the other hand, truth is an ideal point of reference to turn towards in the process of initiatic betterment. Truth is an extreme case which he will be able to approach gradually without ever reaching it. No mason, therefore, can claim he possesses the truth. If he did so, he would be conferring the contents of the revelation on the notion of truth, and consequently, reducing Freemasonry to the state of a religion. But as I will show in Chapter 6 Freemasonry is not a religion.

The same difference in the way of understanding the transcendent can be found if we examine the realisation of the concrete historical project. The difference concerns the way in which the Christian and the mason must behave in the light of it. The Christian must direct his efforts to the realisation of a project in the knowledge that it involves collaborating with Christ in order to be able to achieve salvation, The mason however sees in the concrete historical project a valence of gradual approach to the transcendent, without ever reaching it.

In masonic tradition, transcendence finds expression in the phrase *The Great Architect Of The Universe* (T.G.A.O.T.U.). But is T.G.A.O.T.U. an ontological reality or a simple regulative ideal? While leaving any further examination and definitive clarification of this to the chapter on the relationship between Freemasonry and religion, it is still worth noting even now that the interpretation of T.G.A.O.T.U. as a regulative principle is particularly important for the masonic conception. On the one hand to postulate T.G.A.O.T.U. as a regulative principle means not excluding a priori that he may be identified as the god of some religion. T.G.A.O.T.U. thus becomes the image that the mason creates of the divinity which, in each religion, takes on this or that feature. On the other hand, to consider T.G.A.O.T.U. as a regulative principle allows for a safeguarding the demands of transcendence against the dangers of a naturalistic reduction of the Supreme Being to pure immanence.

According to masonic conception, the principle of transcendence has a dual function:

1 it justifies morals and attributes sense to human reality.
2 it represents the ultimate goal towards which man directs his steps in the continual realisation of his ideals.

Transcendence regulates the immanent, whereas the immanent tends towards transcendence; this is a continual process in which the immanent does not absorb the transcendent, but realises maximum transcendence in itself.

The profane fundamental concepts of Freemasonry (Freedom, Tolerance, Brotherhood, Transcendence) are essential elements in masonic philosophical anthropology, that is they are basic to an understanding of how man is conceived according to Freemasonry. For want of a technical expression let us say that they represent a set of four elements which we call a "quadruple" and which we will specify as *Freedom, Tolerance, Brotherhood and Transcendence.*

One of the first things we must ask ourselves here is do these concepts give a full definition of the constituent elements of masonic anthropology? The answer is decidedly no. We can complete the constituent parts of masonic anthropology by adding another element to the four we already know—the initiatic secret (the fundamental initiatic concept). Thus we have a quintuple) *Freedom, Tolerance, Brotherhood, Transcendence and the Initiatic Secret*—as a full representation of masonic philosophical anthropology.I would like to focus on an important feature in the distinction between philosophical anthropology based on the first four elements and masonic philosophical anthropology itself. The elements of the quadruple *Freedom, Tolerance, Brotherhood, Transcendence* are objective values which those who are not masons can hold. This means that such values, as they are globally understood, do not represent the specific nature of Freemasonry. They express so to speak, its profane counterpart which features in the constituent elements of masonic philosophical anthropology, but only partially. The move to philosophical anthropology *tout court* is accomplished by adding the initiatic secret to the quadruple. But what does that mean? It means that the *overall sense* of masonic philosophical anthropology is only acquired through the rite ofinitiation when one becomes a mason. Here lies a profound and fundamental difference between an initiatic society and any other: whereas the concept of man in a non-initiatic society is recognised by all (we have only to think of Christianity), the conception of man in masonic terms can only be grasped by masons. The initiatic secret, which allows one to reach full cognitive awareness, now takes on an additional meaning by shedding a new light on the quadruple—*Freedom, Tolerance, Brotherhood, Transcendence*—and by giving it an even deeper significance.

The quintuple—*Freedom, Tolerance, Brotherhood, Transcendence, and the Initiatic Secret*—must be taken as a whole. This means that if there were one missing, then there would no longer be this kind of philosophical anthropology. Anyone wishing to deprive masonic philosophical anthropology of either freedom, tolerance, brotherhood, transcendence or the initiatic secret, would not just be weakening or limiting its validity, but rather annulling Freemasonry itself. From this kind of masonic anthropology emerges a man who can improve himself if and only if he satisfies in a unique and personal manner *all the conditions* of the quintuple by which he is formed.

The quintuple expresses a vision of man and of life which should be valid for all men. In this way, it presents itself as an overall conception of man (however susceptible this may be of being integrated with other values). Its aim can only be that of uniting under the starry sky of the Temple all members of the chain of Brotherhood.

In order to further clarify the ideas expressed so far I will go on to explain what is meant by philosophical anthropology.

When man asks himself 'What is man?' and looks to philosophical anthropology for an answer, he wants information on his own nature, his place in the world and the sense of his being. Even the empirical sciences such as psychology, sociology, biology, ethnology, economics and the like, can give a ready answer. How then does philosophical anthropology differ from these sciences? Such sciences have the capacity to provide strict information on the partial aspects of man, yet they are not able to express any global comprehension of him. They contribute towards philosophical anthropology but cannot take its place, because it is the task of philosophical anthropology itself to consider man in his *totality*. One might suppose that this totality is due to a synthetic image created by collecting all the results obtained from scientific investigation of man. In this case one ought to identify a unitary principle capable of giving some order to numerous scientifically valid single elements. Yet it is not possible to offer any scientific justification for this principle, since its nature is philosophical. And this is where the essential difference between philosophical anthropology and the empirical sciences that investigate man lies. Whereas the former exists in order to give a global response to the question 'What is man?', the latter may not even pose this question, which transcends the very limits of scientific investigation. Thus, while the empirical sciences deal with partial and limited aspects of man, it is the task of philosophical anthropology alone to give a total comprehension of him. It is obvious that, in order to express such totality, philosophical anthropology should avail itself of the results the empirical sciences have obtained. Yet in respect to them, it preserves its autonomy of investigation, since the pre-established aim may not be reached by scientific means. Philosophical anthropology is a base which gives sense to each single human experience, i.e. it provides the horizon of totality within which man understands himself and reaches self-fulfilment.

Let us then consider man in his relationship to the world at large. He is born and grows up in a world full of other men and things, a world which on the one hand enriches him but on the other conditions him. His physical life is subjected to the law of physics, chemistry and biology, while his social life–characterised by his relationship to others with whom he shares customs, language and culture–is modelled on the basis of such factors.

Since man belongs to the pre-existing world (of men and things) and is conditioned by it, his development and maturity derive from—though are not confined to—this world. Man is not determined by the outside world in a purely passive manner: he is not just an object but also a subject of the world to which he belongs. Man is not a mere reflection of external reality. Rather, he is capable of expressing his judgement and views on this reality. What is more, he intervenes in the world through his will and action. On the basis of the unity and totality of this dialectic rapport between himself and the world, the conditions of man's external life are related in his mind to an historical and contingent perspective. Naturally the numerous and varied manifestations of social, economic and political life influence man's form of thought and his conception of life, but the way he acts in the world does not depend on these alone. This is why a philosophical anthropology is not just the result of what each empirical science has to say. It must consider that not only is man an observer of reality (in his cognitive function) but he is also a subject endowed with a free will as well as a bearer of values in respect of which scientific knowledge is at least an outsider.

This, in brief then, offers a general justification of the notion of philosophical anthropology and of the reason why masonic thinking can also express its own specific anthropology on the basis of the quintuple, *Freedom, Tolerance, Brotherhood, Transcendence and the Initiatic Secret.* The reader is referred to Chapters 6 and 7 where this anthropology is characterised in relation to others.

Now we must ask ourselves whether the analysis we have carried out so far in the field of masonic anthropology sufficiently characterises the requisites that a mason must satisfy as a *member* of Freemasonry understood as a society of men. The answer is clearly 'No'. The conception of man maintained by Freemasonry must be integrated with a complex of rules to which a mason is subjected on his initiation. These rules include the obligation to adhere to the masonic conception of man, but they must not end there. In masonic anthropology the idea is to make clear the constituent properties of the image of man according to masonic thought. This is a matter of explaining those rules which come to form the human subject as someone belonging to the practical social context provided by masonic society.

In the sense that they belong to the social practical context of Freemasonry as an initiatic society, the constitutive rules for a mason can be summarised as follows:

1 a constituent authority
2 the acceptance of masonic anthropology
3 the swearing of the oath not to divulge the initiatic secret.

The above three requisites are satisfied altogether during the rite of initiation. In fact it is through his initiation that a profane candidate becomes a mason. In the initiation rite, the authority (requisite 1) is represented by the Worshipful Master, while the Candidate accepts the principles maintained by Freemasonry (requisite 2) in the presence of T.G.A.O.T.U. and swears never to disclose the initiation secret (requisite 3). After the oath the Worshipful Master recites the ritualistic formula: 'I name and proclaim you Entered Apprentice of the Freemasons'. From that very instant the Candidate becomes a mason. The constitutive act of the Worshipful Master gives the mason a dimension that only death can dissolve. Even if circumstances in life lead him to stray from masonic principles, he would be considered to be *sleeping*. This means that the masonic dimension will never leave him and he will never be able to reject it. A mason can never return to his former state—he can never become an ex-mason—but simply becomes a mason *asleep*.

After initiation the neophyte becomes part of the worldwide community of masons and collaborates with them all in building the ideal Temple of Brotherhood. At this stage in our investigation it is important to clarify the concept of masonic activity that each mason possesses in a social context. We have seen that all candidates for initiation are presented with the same identical concept of man and with the same initiatic procedure. Thus after initiation each mason finds himself upholding the entire weight of his subjectivity. Each and every one will be a unique and unrepeatable rough stone which will never find its like among others. Consequently, every mason will follow his own path in realising perfection. The smoothing of the rough stone will be carried out by means of the infinite aspects of his subjectivity. This is how, after an identical constitutive act for all, the differences between each individual mason develop. There are masons who are more or less just, good, loyal and so on. In realising the conception of man that he has spontaneously accepted, each mason sets out in front of him freedom, tolerance, brotherhood, transcendence and the initiation secret, bearing the whole burden of his *uniqueness* and *subjectivity*. Thus his self-realisation is accomplished through a continual process oriented by masonic philosophical anthropology and by the ruling principle of The Great Architect of the Universe.

Chapter 3

The Symbols of Freemasonry

The fundamental concepts of Freemasonry are expressed by means of symbols. So for example, the concepts of 'moral law', 'brotherhood' and 'rectitude' are realised in the symbols of 'the book of the Sacred Law' (which would typically be a Bible or a Koran or whatever book expresses a mason's personal faith) 'the compasses' and 'the square'. The symbols 'book', 'compass' and 'square' correspond symbolically to the three Great Lights of the Temple: 'the light above us', 'the light around us' and 'the light within us'. The three Great Lights correspond to other symbols and so on. Thus the ideal Temple is a coherent system of symbols. Each symbol is closely related to all the others and together they give great meaning to initiatic activity. But what functions do the symbols perform? Man has always turned to symbols in his attempt to express his own vision of the world and life, both in a magical and a rational perspective. We have only to think of the profound significance of the Cross in the origins and development of Christianity, or of the 'life' symbol for the ancient Egyptians. And it is through symbols that man has also expressed the most abstract forms of his intellect. Generally speaking we can distinguish two categories of symbols: those which denote conceptual abstractions and those which have a prevalently allegorical role. The symbols of logic and mathematics belong to the first category, while the complex of signs whose function is to represent in a sensitive manner the ideal contents that are not completely exhausted by our capacity of knowledge, belong to the second.

In order to be able to explain the capacity of logical and mathematical symbolism, let us consider the following elementary algebraic expression $x^2-y^2=(x+y)(x-y)$ and try to express it without using the variables x and y, the brackets and the plus and minus signs. What we would obtain would be the following proposition. 'The result of subtracting the square of a number from the square of another gives the same number obtained by adding the two numbers, subtracting the first from the second, and then multiplying the results of the two operations'. Clearly the symbolic expression presents certain advantages in respect to the literal one: it is shorter, clearer and more precise. Furthermore it overcomes all the difficulties of the different languages in which literal expressions are formulated. Logicians and mathematicians of different countries can communicate on the basis of a universal use of symbols. A logical and mathematical formula has the same meaning in different times and spaces, in different cultures and languages. Nevertheless, man has always been hindered more or less deeply, and more or less explicitly, in his acceptance of the use of symbols. This may be due to the effort needed to learn to comprehend the concept of symbols and to make correct use of them, or to a psychological resistance to abstract reasoning, or to the difficulty in being able to 'see' immediately what the symbols express.

These characteristics of logical and mathematical symbols are more noticeable in symbols expressing allegories. Before examining the symbols of Freemasonry it is necessary to dispose of some widely held fallacies:

First: that it has always been one of the main tasks of Freemasonry to plot against Church and State. Its symbols are no more than a cover for such destructive plots.

Second: that Freemasonry does not have a single original thought to offer: the symbols perform the role of creating illusions for its members of some grandiose but non-existent plan.

Third: that Freemasonry exists for the financial benefit of its members: the symbols are used simply to deceive non-masons.

Fourth: that the symbols of Freemasonry are a useless complication which makes the work of 'smoothing the rough stone' more difficult. Those who support these ideas contend that the symbols should be abolished.

Those masons who search the symbols for lost esoteric truths, ancient wisdoms, the secrets of alchemy and the philosopher's stone are against their abolition. But the symbols are weak and barely capable, even superficially, of expressing the profound meanings of the esoteric life of man.

These and other interpretations of masonic symbolism are wrong and thus incapable of capturing its real nature. This can be encapsulated as follows: in Freemasonry the symbols express one secret, the initiation secret. There is only one initiation, which consists of seeing oneself as a link in the ideal chain of brotherhood. Anyone incapable of understanding this will always be in the position of the profane who happens to walk into a masonic Temple and observes objects familiar to him such as the square, compass, mallet and book, but cannot understand their symbolic meaning. In order to 'read' what he sees, he needs masonic light which can only be granted to him through initiation. Only then will he understand the masonic secret and become part of a new moral dimension, entering into a symbolic union with others to whom the same secret has been revealed. It is this very symbolism that represents the foundation common to all masonic circles throughout the world. By learning the symbols and allegories which they express, the mason is in a position to understand the supreme principles of Universal Freemasonry, whatever the language and in the simplest way possible. When a mason enters a Temple anywhere in the world he can take part in the initiatic works whatever the language or culture.

Through its use of symbols Freemasonry manages to speak, regardless of historical contingencies, a unique and universal language, reflecting the characteristic of immutability. Indeed, once the basic thought has been formulated in symbols, it is transmitted without any substantial modification. In this way a continuity of tradition is guaranteed. Consequently the mason of today performs his initiatic work just as did a mason of 250 years ago. Any differences are a result of the changing conditions of history. From this point of view, the problems which the mason faces today are no different from those he had to solve in the past. The conception of man maintained by Freemasonry cannot change, but its contingent manifestations follow the unfolding of history.

Initiatic work, which is both everlasting and historical, is not carried out by each individual mason, but rather by the community of men who share the same principles and ideals of Freemasonry. In the Temple each mason smooths his rough stone in collaboration with other masons. Thus each mason is a link in the chain of the Brotherhood: just as a chain cannot exist without its individual links, so the links, taken one by one, cannot form a chain. Both the chain and the single links are therefore essential to each other.

This last reflection highlights a second aspect regarding the essential nature of symbolism in masonic practice. In its purely metaphorical role, symbolism is closely connected to the initiatic secret. One cannot be initiated into this secret without the use of symbolism, since to be initiated means embarking upon a practical process of betterment that the candidate can take up only if he understands the symbolic and ritual significance of its stages.

In conclusion, symbolism is a consequence of Freemasonry being an initiatic society. The oath, which we considered in Chapter 2 to be an essential requisite for entering Freemasonry, concerns the initiation secret. Thus symbolism as an instrument of expression of the initiatic secret, and the oath as a commitment not to transgress it, represent the line of demarcation between Freemasonry and any other non-initiatic society. If the secret is disclosed and destructured from its symbolism, the foundations of Freemasonry immediately come to nothing. A Masonic circle without any initiatic foundation is nothing but an ordinary society with philanthropic aims.

In conclusion to this chapter, I wish to try to find an answer (albeit partial and imprecise) to the question 'What are the origins of the symbols that characterise masonic thought today?' It seems to me that nearly all human civilisations have supposedly attributed to Freemasonry a wealth of legends, allegories and symbols. We need think no further than the ancient world in which the Egyptians, Assyrians and Greeks (Pythagoras in particular) communicated their scientific and religious knowledge by resorting to symbolic expressions (rational and allegorical) and according to an initiatic procedure. In the centuries that followed, the first editions of the Bible represented an endless source of wealth of masonic symbolism (*vide* the legends concerning the building and rebuilding of Solomon's Temple and the corresponding symbols that still adorn masonic symbolism today). The manuscripts of Ancient Charges which characterise the period between 1390 and 1700, throw some light on the activity of operative masons but curiously enough use few symbolic expressions. On the other hand it appears that the main source of masonic symbolism is to be found in the tradition of alchemy, not only as far as fundamental notions such as 'the regeneration of man' and 'the secret' are concerned, but also with regard to such symbols as 'the serpent eating its tail' (an expression of eternity and divine wisdom), 'the compass', 'the square', 'the rule', 'the perfect ashlar', 'the pillars', 'the balance', 'the five-pointed star', 'the six-pointed star', 'the triangle' (the sacred delta), 'the double-headed eagle' and so on. We can therefore affirm that most of the symbolism of speculative Freemasonry is the expression of learned men who came into Freemasonry in the seventeenth and eighteenth centuries and transformed its symbolism by employing their deep knowledge of alchemical thought.

Chapter 4

A Masonic Lay Morality

I have already claimed that morality represents the highest point in the spiritual life of man and that it is justified by a transcendent regulative principle (the Great Architect of the Universe), which gives meaning to reality as it is understood in masonic terms. It is also the goal towards which the initiatic work of the mason aspires. I propose to develop these notions further by beginning to reflect further on the nature of morality.

We noted earlier that freedom is the foundation of morality; without freedom, there is no morality. The freedom we are referring to, however, is not a simple capacity of choice but rather the capacity to adhere to an objective order of values. A capacity, that is, to follow the moral norms that are derived from such values. From this point of view morality imposes a constraint on freedom. But of what does this constraint consist? To understand it correctly we must examine a phenomenon which belongs to the fundamental experiences of human existence. In our daily lives we experience values which are to be recognised and realised, obligations which force us to sacrifice things that are attractive to us and consequently impose constraints on freedom, even though they appeal to our free decision. We are speaking of a phenomenon of morality to which philosophers of all times have devoted their energies. But what do we mean by moral value? From an historical point of view, we find that in every society, from the most primitive to the most developed, man's actions are judged good or bad, just or unjust, to be praised or condemned. On a historical level we are witness to a relativism of normative concepts; what is good for some may be bad for others. Yet beyond all the contingent differentiations there emerges a general principle on the basis of which man distinguishes good from bad. This principle derives from an original fact, from a universal human fundamental experience, which finds complete expression in the concept of moral good. But what is the moral good that constrains freedom?

From an approximative idea, we must take into consideration some proposals which have been formulated by renowned thinkers. In a first attempt at finding a meaning, moral good is *reduced* to other types of good. What is pleasant, useful, etc. is morally good, where pleasant and useful are values expressing a practical end. Thus moral good is relativized and at the same time loses its own independence and state of conditioning. Moral good becomes a means for different ends. This is only a partial explanation of moral good, since very often moral obligation requires renouncing what is useful and pleasant. In this case, what is useful and pleasant is not representive of moral good but rather of its opposite.

Secondly, moral good is not considered with respect to the practical aims to which it can be related but with respect to its causes. By this we mean mainly social causes. The capacity to express value judgements appears to derive from the type of education that one receives in a given society, where a certain way of conceiving what is good and bad, just and unjust is prevalent. Man acts according to what is good or what is bad, following the particular conception of morality present in the society in which he lives. While undoubtedly capturing something that contributes to the formation of morality in man, it is, like the previous meaning, only partial. It cannot override the fact that, apart from social change, there are certain fundamental moral necessities that cannot be suppressed. This means that we must search for the nature of morality elsewhere, and that the two above-mentioned meanings of moral good are the result of a partial interpretation of moral phenomena. Therefore we will return to our first question on the meaning of moral good.

So far, we appear to have established that one requisite must be satisfied in order to characterise moral good, or rather, the impossibility of reducing it to partial forms of good. The two preceding meanings fail to capture this fundamental aspect for the very reason that they are partial and relative. Consequently we must look elsewhere. First of all what do we mean by good? Let us say that it is anything that reflects the realisation of a value, even if partial. Good is good in that it refers to some values and for man supreme value is constituted by its realisation. Man is not born perfect but in the course of his existence he acquires various levels that are ever expanding towards perfection. Various scales of values correspond to these various levels. We move from biological values to more articulated and differentiated ones—economic, aesthetic, civil, etc. Moral good consists in realising maximum good with a view to reaching a complete realisation of man. Whereas other values make man a good student, a good lawyer, a good doctor, a good husband and so on, moral values are typical of man in his capacity as man. All those actions which are directed towards the realisation of man in his entirety are good: what conforms to the realisation of his nature is morally good, whereas all that is in opposition to it is morally bad. Moral value thus comes to include all other values: biological, economic, practical, artistic, cultural, etc. Moral value is not a partial value like all other values, but it expresses the point of view of a global consideration of them: all that is morally good is so if viewed in relation to the totality of its dimensions. What is more, this totality must be considered in its finality. Indeed, the aim of moral good is the realisation of man, for which reason, by representing this realisation as a task man directs himself towards in a continual upward path, the aim of moral good becomes a transcendent end that man approaches in a process of approximation in the immanent.

This dynamic process, which in Freemasonry is effected on the basis of the constituent elements of the quintuple *Freedom, Tolerance, Brotherhood, Transcendence, The Initiatic Secret*, is expressed in the sense that it is oriented by man towards a continual surpassing and perfecting of the self, which brushes the top of immanence on the moral plane, and is regulated by the ideal principle of transcendence in the figure of The Great Architect of the Universe. One might wonder whether the foundation of morality is placed in man or in The Great Architect of the Universe. A number of people support the first theory: we have only to think, for example, of the basic view of the Grand Orient of France which, by eliminating The Great Architect of the Universe, placed the foundation of morality in the immanence of man's conscience. As I have already had occasion to stress in Chapter 2, I firmly believe that transcendence is an essential requisite for Freemasonry. Without The Great Architect of the Universe, it is not possible to justify the objective validity of human morality. In actual fact, The Great Architect of the Universe and man are two aspects bound together in an essential and indestructible knot: man can be the bearer of an authentic moral dimension only if he is seen in his relation to the supreme and absolute, represented by The Great Architect of the Universe, whereas The Great Architect of the Universe himself may become the foundation of morality only if he is thought of in concrete terms as an end towards which man is directed. This is how the unconditional state of moral values can be understood, it is justified and found in the regulative ideal of T.G.A.O.T.U. Without this foundation, moral values would be relative just as all other values are and thus incapable of realising the complete perfection of man.

It is not difficult to see that the idea of T.G.A.O.T.U. is the key to masonic thinking. Indeed, it is at the root of the masonic conception of morality, where T.G.A.O.T.U. is understood as a transcendent principle, a guarantee for moral values and an ideal destination to be reached along the road of ethics. This is why it is not possible to treat the problem of morality in masonic thinking without closely analysing the nature of T.G.A.O.T.U. and the various views that have been adopted in the course of masonic history around the figure that T.G.A.O.T.U. represents. Let us return to the distinction between operative and speculative Freemasonry we formulated which in Chapter 1. The God of the operative masons was the Christian God in the ontological sense. This seems clear if we remember that, whereas the role of the Church was to control the work of the cathedral builders, their sole source of inspiration was the Christian religion in all its different manifestations, ancient and modern. In short, T.G.A.O.T.U. was the Christian God. There are still Lodges that work operatively and identify transcendence with the Christian God.

The situation changed radically in the speculative phase of Freemasonry, coincident with its modern origins. Admission into the Temple of the 'accepted', (i.e. those with ideals often contrary to dogmatism and orthodoxy) predisposed newly born speculative Freemasonry to the influence of deism. The Constitutions of Anderson (see Chapter 5) accepted deism and placed it at the base of the idea of T.G.A.O.T.U. Anderson replaced the Christian religion, the expression of a particular faith, with the universal Religion of deism. He did no more than replace one religion with another.

Freemasonry no longer took inspiration from Christianity, but from deism. (Christianity and deism are understood here in their ontological sense—regulativism is still a long way off).

Since deism characterises the modern origins and the early development of Freemasonry in the world, it is worth pausing for a moment to explain its fundamental principles, although these will be dealt with more fully in Chapter 6.

The term 'deism', in all its various meanings, essentially points to a natural religion based on reason. In fact it maintains that the aim of religion is morality and that all that is conceived beyond morality is superfluous. Consequently deism is presented as a religious conception having an underlying purpose towards immanentism in human life. Furthermore every man has the right to his own opinion on all aspects of reality and the right to pass on these thoughts to those men in whom the same right is recognised with a view to aiming for a general common goal. Deism therefore becomes the presupposition of tolerance which finds expression in the revolt against orthodoxy and dogmatism. This is where the most significant aspect of deism lies; because it derives from a revolt against the authority of religion, it becomes the banner waved in the fight for political and social reform. In fact deism inspired the American Revolution, the French Revolution and Frederick the Great's liberal reforms in Germany.

The term 'deism' was first adopted by Pierre Viret, in his work, *Instruction Chrétienne* published in 1564. He proposed to attribute to this term a meaning quite the opposite of atheism. 'Deism' remained unknown as a term in England until 1621, the year in which it appeared in Burton's *Anatomy of Melancholy* with the same meaning understood by Viret. It was not until 1682 in Dryden's preface to his poem *Religio Laici* that it was used to characterise natural religion.

Deism was first manifested in its sense of natural religion in Great Britain, by certain philosophers who, far from forming a school of thought, were individualists, often unknown to each other and at times, with differing views. The father of the English deists was Lord Herbert of Cherbury (1583-1648) who formulated the common notions which were to establish the rational base of deism. Since they were universal notions, they could be shared by all men and made known through reason. Consequently, albeit not explicitly, revelation was rejected. After Lord Herbert, the most famous English deists were Toland (1670-1722) Collins (1676-1729) and Tindal (1657-1733), whose works were well known both at home and abroad.

Deism spread in France and with it Illuminism. The most authoritative French deist was Voltaire (1694-1778) who propounded the idea of a natural religion based on reason while condemning all forms of tyranny, dogmatism and superstition. Jean Jacques Rousseau accepted deism, even if not in such a clear form as Voltaire. Deism was also a source of inspiration for such philosophers as d'Alembert, Diderot, Baron d'Holbach, Helvetius, La Mettrie, Condillac and Condorcet who strengthened the immanent vision of human life by expressing an almost blind faith in the constant and inevitable progress of man and society. Although strongly influenced by English deism, deism in France tended to be both politically and religiously more radical and extreme. This was due to the different political and economical conditions of the two societies. Whereas in England social progress was a reality, in France the authoritarian State led people to a state of exasperation, thus creating the ideological and material conditions for the Revolution.

In Germany, Illuminism manifested itself differently than in England and France. Under the influence of Leibniz and

Wolff, a rational naturalism prevailed which not only greatly influenced philosophical thinking during the reign of Frederick the Great, but political and social life as well. The *Aufklärung* did not assume the radical forms it did in French Illuminism. Apart from Lessing the most important German deists were Bahrdt, Eberhard and Edelmann.

European deism made its way to the English colonies in America where it spread rapidly. These ideas were professed by Franklin, Jefferson, Washington and Allen and became the spiritual bond of the Fathers of the Revolution.

It is then easy to see then how deism developed in the western world alongside the spread of Freemasonry. In England, France, Germany and the United States it was identified with Freemasonry: the most influential masons were deists. This is clear from the fact that the Constitutions of Anderson, which were affected by deism, were accepted by masons all over the world. For Anderson and the Grand Lodge of London deism clearly meant a release from dogmatism and orthodoxy, as well as a justification for the principle of tolerance which is essential to the very life of Freemasonry. Freedom of thought and tolerance are such fundamental gifts that they are accepted in the deistic vision of human life. Placed at the roots of modern Freemasonry, deism thus helped it to spread rapidly throughout the world, wherever elected spirits saw in the enlightenment of reason the force needed to drag mankind out from the millennial sleep of intolerance and oppression.

However, deism brought about a deep rupture in English Freemasonry. Many influential masons believed that an authentic masonic tradition infused with Christianity was 'betrayed' by the immanentistic interpretation of deism. A rupture between Antients and Moderns was inevitable. The act of reconciliation from which the United Grand Lodge of

England originates marked, among other things, the superceding of deism by a concept according to which the Great Architect of the Universe is a personal God, separate from the world and active in it.

In this way T.G.A.O.T.U. is attributed a valence tending more towards transcendence: deism is replaced by theism. But which theism? Theism is a term with more than one meaning. So which meaning is specific to Freemasonry? Obviously more than one interpretation can be accepted as valid, otherwise it would oppose the characteristics of modern Freemasonry which, having accepted the principle of tolerance, respects all religions. Furthermore a rejection of dogmatism quashes the ancient belief in the Christian God held by operative masons. The only valid interpretation for theism in a masonic view is, in my opinion, the interpretation which derives from the regulative conception of T.G.A.O.T.U. By considering T.G.A.O.T.U. as a transcendent regulative principle, the immanentistic and naturalistic conception is more easily overcome since T.G.A.O.T.U. orientates the immanent without being absorbed by it, and absolves masons from the obligation of having to take up a precise position as far as religion is concerned. This last point regarding the relationship between Freemasonry and religion will be dealt with more fully from a theoretical point of view in Chapter 6.

Chapter 5

Masonic Constitutions

In Chapter 2 we spoke of the three basic requirements a man has to satisfy in order to become a mason. He must accept the authority that makes him such, share masonic anthropology and swear he will never reveal the initiation secret. Furthermore, there are obligations and particular rules that regulate the way in which these requisites must be satisfied from an historical point of view, and consequently, that reflect the codification on a formal level of the masonic institution. These complex rules and obligations are defined in the masonic Constitutions, whose function is to define

1. the constituent authority
2. the principles of philosophical anthropology that must be infused in the mason
3. the modalities of the oath regarding the initiatic secret.

The modern Constitutions of Freemasonry were drawn up by Anderson in 1723 and later modified by him in 1738. No further official modifications of these Constitutions were ever made, in spite of numerous interpretations and applications following historical changes and other contingencies of both a geographical and national nature. However any change (and possible official codification of this change) caused problems of both a theoretical and practical nature. As far as the former is concerned, it is clear that the Constitutions had to be modified according to the constituent authority, the principles of masonic philosophical anthropology and the modalities of the oath. Within Freemasonry no-one can ever accept that any radical change may be made in respect to these three different areas. However numerous historical and cultural interpretations have been attributed to them, both in a synchronic and diachronic sense. Yet all these variants are seen as being due more to the historical conditioning that Freemasonry has been subjected to than to a real process of transformation of its constituent principles. There may well have been a deeper transformation in the area of anthropology as I will try to show later. Returning to the Constitutions of Anderson, I will demonstrate how they represent the moment of official coding of deistic thought and therefore the initial moment of that orientation which brought Freemasonry to a more or less conscious acceptance of naturalistic theism.

Since the conception of the Supreme Being underwent a great transformation within masonic circles from the *Act of Union* of 1813, in which a choice was made in favour of theism, (however much this choice was conceptually ambiguous), I will try to show that the Constitutions should be revised on this point. By re-examining the Constitutions of Anderson, we will also be able to emphasise that, in spite of these modifications, Freemasonry evolves more in the sense of its concepts and principles being clarified, with a consequent definition of a regulatively definitive formal order, than in the sense of a transformism dictated by opportuneness and historical conditioning.

Let us take a look at the Constitutions of Anderson in their origins and fundamental principles.

On September 20th 1721, the Grand Lodge of London entrusted James Anderson with the task of reformulating the ancient Constitutions. Before that time each Lodge had its own Constitutions with its own fundamental maxims. There were also some manuscripts, a number of which were very old. The Grand Master, the Duke of Montagu, asked fourteen brothers to examine Anderson's work, which they approved making only slight modifications. On 17th January 1723 the Grand Lodge ordered that it should be published and a book appeared entitled *The Constitutions of Free-masons, Containing the History, Charges, Regulations, etc. of that Most Ancient and Right Worshipful Fraternity.* The historical compendium and ancient charges were the work of Anderson while the general rules were compiled by George Payne and two other dignitaries.

It is worth noting that the Constitutions of Anderson were issued by the Grand Lodge, that is by an authority higher than the individual Lodges. The idea of creating a Grand Lodge whose task was to judge the regularity and constitutions of the Lodges, seems to have originated so as to avoid the danger inherent in admitting 'accepted' brothers into the Lodges, of alienating the spirit and tradition of Freemasonry. In any case, the institution of the Grand Lodge marks an event that was born at the same time as modern Freemasonry and is still today one of its most important aspects. The existence of a Grand Lodge undoubtedly limited the autonomy of the individual Lodges, at least to the extent to which they were controlled. In a few extreme cases, they were closed if they did not correspond to the criteria of regularity formulated by the Grand Lodge through the Constitutions and Rituals. On the other hand the idea of the Grand Lodge has penetrated so deeply into masonic tradition in the last 250 years that it seems impossible to do without it.

The chapter in the Constitutions of Anderson on the charges of a mason is particularly important. Anderson based his work on the ancient Crafts that had belonged to Freemasonry since the fifteenth century and perhaps even earlier. The first versions of these Crafts, together with a Traditional History, have been handed down to us in two texts, the Regius MS and the concluding parts of the MS known as the Cooke Text. The first part of this text consists of a history that was probably written in the 15th century and elaborated in the 16th, while the second concerns the Crafts whose separate clauses were re-organised into a Code of General and Special Charges, which Henry VI is supposed to have approved. From the 16th century onwards, the majority of the manuscripts contained a transcription of the History and Code of Henry VI with textual variations named Ancient Charges. The different versions of the Ancient Charges can be grouped together into five families, known as Plot, Grand Lodge, Sloane, Roberts and Spencer. Anderson referred to these documents when he affirmed in the heading of the Constitutions that his Charges were taken from ancient documents. Ever since, the heading 'Constitutions' has been understood as the Regulations issued by the Grand Lodge and we find it in 17th and 18th century versions in the Grand Lodge, Sloane and Roberts groups, generally in the plural but occasionally in the singular.

The chapter entitled 'The General Heads of the Charges of a Free-Mason' contains the following headings: I Of God and Religion, II Of the Civil Magistrate, Supreme and Subordinate, III Of Lodges, IV Of Masters, Wardens, Fellows, and Apprentices, V Of the Management of the Craft in Working, VI Of Behaviour. The first, second and sixth of these headings are particularly significant for us here.

In discussing the Charges of a mason towards God and Religion, the ancient texts affirmed that he was to be faithful to God and to the Holy Church, lest he should fall into bad ways or commit heresy. The first Charge of Anderson proposed that this should be enlarged upon and substantially modified. In fact, it read as follows:

A mason is obliged, by his tenure, to obey the moral law; and if he rightly understands the Art, he will never be a stupid atheist, nor an irreligious libertine. But though in ancient times masons were charged in every Country to be of the Religion of that Country or Nation, whatever it was, yet now it is thought more expedient only to oblige them to that Religion in which all men agree, leaving their particular opinions to themselves; that is to be good men and true, or men of honour and honesty, by whatever denominations or persuasions they may be distinguished; whereby Freemasonry becomes the center of union, and the means of conciliating true friendship among persons that must have remained at a perpetual distance.

This Charge contains the phrase 'yet now it is thought more expedient only to oblige them to that Religion in which all men agree, leaving their particular opinions to themselves', which reflects the principle foundation of deism which inspired Anderson. Today it is surprising that the Grand Lodge of London who issued the Constitutions was accused of irreligiosity. In order to avoid controversy on this and other points, it followed the example of the Royal Society and prohibited any discussion of religion and politics by declaring the sixth Charge. However, as I have already shown in the first chapter, this veto could not avoid a deep split in English Freemasonry, with the consequent opposition of the Moderns to the Antients and the creation of the Grand Lodge of England. Deism then, was at the root of this division between English masons, reflecting a particular way of conceiving religion that was not shared by all and sundry. It is true that in taking inspiration from deism, the Grand Lodge of London sided with the more illustrious spirits against the dogmatism of the churches, affirming that religion could no longer serve to divide men and set them against each other as irreconcilable enemies. In this way it played an important and positive role in making modern Freemasonry the propelling element of the more illustrious intellectuals of the eighteenth century. On the other hand, the criticisms of the Antients held a profound truth in the principle of transcendence that prevailed only in the 19th century (subsequent to the Act of Union in 1813) and gave masonic thought an order that is still valid today.

The second Charge affirms:

A mason is a peaceable subject to the Civil Powers, wherever he resides or works, and is never to be concerned in plots and conspiracies against the peace and welfare of the Nation, nor to behave himself undutifully to inferior magistrates; for as Freemasonry has been always injured by war, bloodshed, and confusion. so ancient Kings and Princes have been much disposed to encourage the Craftsmen, because of their peacebleness and loyalty, whereby they practically answered the cavils of their adversaries, and promoted the honour of the Fraternity, who ever flourished in times of peace. So that if a Brother should be a rebel against the State, he is not to be countenanced in his rebellion, however he may be pitied as an unhappy man, and, if convicted of no other crime, though the loyal Brotherhood must and ought to disown his rebellion, and give no umbrage or ground of political jealousy to the Government for the time being; they cannot expel him from the Lodge, and his relation to it remains indefeasible.

This Charge contains a principal affirmation, that is 'a Mason is a peaceable subject to the Civil Powers'. It also contains a clause on the basis of which 'if a Brother should be a rebel, and if convicted of no other crime, he cannot be expelled from the Lodge'. This clause reflects a compromise between two opposing tendencies within English Masonry. On the one hand many masons loyally supported the Royal Family of Hanover and George I who personified the traditional element in politics and religion, while others supported the Jacobite, revolutionary tendency. There is then a clear reference to the rebellious brothers and Jacobites who especially needed protection. Even here, in order to avoid criticism of the Craft, political discussion was forbidden on the basis of the sixth Charge which reads:

Therefore no private piques or quarrels must be brought within the door of the Lodge, far less any quarrels about Religion, or Nations, or State policy, we being only, as masons, of the universal Religion above-mentioned.

These Charges were clearly conditioned in their formulation by political and religious contingencies as well as by a shared philosophical anthropology. Such political and religious contingencies are undoubtedly no longer relevant today and therefore need revising.

The Constitutions of Anderson of 1723 were modified by him in 1738. Since the new book of the Constitutions presents some substantial modifications with respect to the first, it is worth comparing it not only with the 1723 version, but also with an interpretation of the latter as it appears in a French document of 1735-36 (MS no FM 146, Bibliothèque Nationale). Here too we will limit our comparison to Charges 1, 2 and 6.

Taking the first Charge regarding God and religion, let us compare the following:

(A) ANDERSON 1723 'A mason is obliged, by his tenure, to obey the moral law; and if he rightly understands the Art, *he will never be* a stupid atheist, *nor an irreligious libertine*'.

(B) ANDERSON 1738 'A mason is obliged, by his tenure, to obey the moral law; and if he rightly understands the Art, he will never be a stupid atheist, nor an irreligious libertine, nor *will he act against the dictates of his conscience*'.

(C) FRENCH DOCUMENT 'A mason is obliged, by his tenure, to obey the moral law; and if he rightly understands the Art, *he will never be* an atheist, nor a *libertine without Religion*'.

In particular, I intend to analyse and compare the expressions in italics. First comparison: (A)-(C). Whereas in the declaration of Anderson in 1723 we read 'a mason...will never be...an *irreligious* libertine', in the French document we read that 'a mason...will never be...a libertine *without religion*'. There is a cosiderable difference between 'not being irreligious' and 'not being without religion'. In fact, whilst irreligiosity is an attitude towards religion and can mean either that *one has* a religion (but one is irreligious) or that *one does not have* a religion (and one is irreligious), the statement that one cannot be without religion has the meaning that one must have (one cannot be without) a religion. Since for the Freemasonry of those times, religion meant the universal religion based on human reason (deism), the French Document is more precise in expressing this notion.

Furthermore it must be stressed that the Constitutions of Anderson of 1738 (B) differed both from the previous version and from the French Document, since they included another condition, that *a mason is bound never to act against the dictates of his conscience*. The reflections resulting from this added condition are important, in that after having declared the necessity of adhering to a universal objective religion on which all men can rationally agree, the *subjective* element of the human conscience is introduced with force. From a philosophical point of view, the global sense attributed to religion is greatly increased, yet recourse to subjectivity may create ambiguity and misunderstanding. In fact an extreme case could be hypothesised in which the same objectivity of universal religion opposed the conscience of the single subject for which, if one's conscience is to make the final decision, it might even decide to refuse objective and universal religion. This case, which can be argued from the Constitutions of Anderson, found concrete realisation in France, when the Grand Orient decided to reject the Grand Architect of the Universe in favour of an appeal to the conscience of each individual mason. It is ironic, to say the least, that such a rejection should have derived from the Constitutions of Anderson, who was an Englishman.

There are no notable differences in the three formulations of the second and third Charges regarding the supreme and subordinate civil magistrate and the behaviour of the masons, respectively.

Before beginning to analyse how Freemasonry is organised into degrees, as it is codified in the Constitutions of Anderson, it is worth briefly mentioning what are known as the 'Landmarks'. The term Landmark as far as Freemasonry is concerned, indicates a line of demarcation beyond which masonic identity is lost. The Landmarks can be correctly understood if they are classified as *ancient* and *modern* with the Constitutions of Anderson acting as the dividing line. Anderson himself speaks of the Landmarks when he establishes, through norm XXXIV of the 'General Regulations', that each Grand Lodge has the power and authority to make new regulations or modify existing ones as long as the ancient Landmarks are faithfully preserved.

A careful and well documented analysis of the modern Landmarks (subsequent to the Constitutions of Anderson) is found in Volume IV of 'The Scottish Temple' to which the reader is referred for further information. Of the fifteen collections of Landmarks considered let me give as an example the one formulated by the Grand Lodge of Connecticut. It comprises of nineteen Landmarks as follows:

1 Belief in the existence of the Supreme Being, in a certain revelation of his will, in the resurrection of the body and in the immortality of the soul.
2 The obligation and means of recognition and the legend of the Third Degree.
3 The teaching of moral virtues, goodwill and doctrines of natural religion, by means of symbols derived from the Temple of King Solomon and his tradition, and from the habits and customs observed and from the instruments and materials used for its construction.
4 That Masons must obey moral law and the government of the country in which they live.
5 That the Grand Master is the head of the Fraternity.
6 That the Worshipful Master is the Head of the Lodge.
7 That the Grand Lodge is the supreme governing body within its territorial jurisdiction.
8 That each Lodge has a natural right to be represented in the Grand Lodge by its three first Officials and their Procurators.
9 That each Lodge has the power to make Masons and administer their own business.
10 That each candidate must be a man who has reached his majority, was born of free parents, is not subjected to restrictions of freedom, and is as strong and healthy as a man should be.
11 That no candidate may be received unless unanimously voted, after due investigation into his merits.
12 That voting is an inviolable secret.
13 That all Masons, as such, are equal.
14 That all Lodges are equal.

15 That all Grand Lodges are equal.
16 That no-one may be installed as Worshipful Master of the Lodge unless he is an ex-Steward, or unless by special dispensation from the Grand Master.
17 That the obligations, means of recognition and the formalities and ceremonies observed in the conferring of degrees are secret.
18 That no innovation may be made in the body of Freemasonry.
19 That the Ancient Landmarks are the supreme law and cannot be changed or repealed.

An examination of the above collections of Landmarks shows some essential characteristics common to all of them, concerning: a) the integration of the Constitutions with contributions of a religious nature; b) a circumscribed destination with consequent limitation of their capacity.

As far as point a) is concerned, an explicit reference is already made to features of the Christian religion in the first Landmark with 'the belief in the existence of a Supreme Being, in a certain revelation of his will, in the resurrection of his body and in the immortality of the soul'. But analagous points are found in other collections too, as will be clear from a reading of the above-mentioned 'Scottish Temple'. With regards to point b) it is evident that the individual listings of Landmarks are an expression of the convictions in which masons are subjected to the authority of a particular Grand Lodge. It is not by chance that in the volume mentioned we find the listings issued by the Grand Lodges of Connecticut, Massachusetts, Kentucky, Nevada, Minnesota, Tennessee, New Jersey, Florida, New York, West Virginia and Vermont. Besides these listings, which are characterised by the fact that they were issued and adopted by a regular jurisdiction, the text also records two listings of Landmarks proposed by individual scholars who were not endowed with the authority that can be conferred by the Grand Lodge. In fact it was through the issue of the Landmarks that the Grand Lodges expressed a very important need to define the everlasting and unchangeable dimension of masonic thought, by fixing a boundary between what is and what is not masonic. However, the results obtained proved insufficient since the different Landmarks included in the listings corresponded to *different interpretations* of masonic thought. In short, the different listings of Landmarks provided *different boundaries* to unique masonic thought. Their insufficiency derives from their number. This is particularly noticeable in those very aspects in which Freemasonry hovers between different positions such as the stand it takes in the face of religion or rituality (we have only to think of the Legend of the Third Degree).

We must now ask whether the Landmarks have an authority equal to that of the Constitutions of Anderson. I believe that the second characteristic of the listings of the Landmarks we made mention of above, was quite an important element in finding an interpretation of the Landmarks and their capacity. Being issued by certain Grand Lodges, the Landmarks transform the convictions shared by all its members into principles of Freemasonry. It is a question of establishing whether these principles are to be understood as *general* principles valid not only for those masons who formulated them but also for all masons. Let us consider those Landmarks which deal with the religious components that are shared by all masons who have to obey a particular Grand Lodge and ask ourselves whether these constitute principles of Freemasonry in general. The answer is no, since certain specific elements of religious dogma (such as, for example, the resurrection of the body) are not necessarily valid for all masons. As I have shown in the previous chapters, one can be a mason without necessarily accepting all the dogma of each specific religion. If, on the other hand, this belief is imposed as an essential requirement to be satisfied before becoming a mason, then the validity of masonic thought comes to be greatly restricted. However, the Landmarks show that belonging to a Lodge does not exclude the possibility of adhering to religious faiths as well, which go beyond masonic thought. The main thing is that the right of the individual mason (as for example, the right to believe in the resurrection of the body) is not to be mistaken for the duty of the mason as such (who is not obliged to believe in the resurrection of the body). This kind of confusion is certainly to be avoided, if one understands masonic thought along the lines I have traced in this book. Therefore, the masonic Constitutions and Landmarks should not be placed on the same level.

Let us return to the Constitutions of Anderson and consider the part played by the three symbolic degrees—Entered Apprentice, Fellow Craft and Master Mason.

There appear to have been one or two degrees before the constitution of the Grand Lodge of London in 1717 (historians have not reached any definite and unequivocable conclusion as to the existence and nature of the second degree). However the articulation of Freemasonry into three degrees was officially recognised in 1738 with the publication of Anderson's Constitutions.

Freemasonry developed in the 18th century, characterised by attempts to give it a definitive and stable order. This is where the problem of the initiatic degrees arose: how many and which degrees constitute the Craft? The answers to these questions were not always unanimous. Some masons felt that three degrees were insufficient, and proposed that other degrees be introduced. Thus the bases were laid down not only for the constitution of the Rites but also for a closer study of the Craft, which among other things, marked the birth of the Royal Arch (cf B E Jones' authoritative work *The Freemason's Book of the Royal Arch* for historical reference to the Royal Arch which I will use in the considerations that follow).

What idea characterises the Royal Arch? In what sense should the term 'arch', be understood? Although different interpretations have been proposed, it seems that the term 'arch' as used in the Freemasonry of the Royal Arch, has an architectonic meaning and symbolises strength, beauty and competence—all necessary elements in its construction. It is built with a series of wedge-shaped stones placed one on top of the other with the first stones placed on either side of a plinth. The other stones are joined with mortar or cement. But the true force that allows the arch to support the enormous weight that bears down on it is given by the keystone at the centre of the vault, which uniformly distributes the weight over the two sides and functions independently of mortar or cement. It is this very arch that becomes a symbol of the Royal Arch.

But what does this symbol express? First we must note that the main aim of the Royal Arch is that of 'remedying a loss'. To understand this, it is worth making mention of the legend of the Royal Arch, which in the English interpretation, concerns the reconstruction of Solomon's Temple. This refers to the chance discovery of an underground crypt on the site of the Temple and the bringing to the light of the Book of the Sacred Law. In the Royal Arch the crypt becomes an arched vault and serves as a theme for its ritual.

The Royal Arch spread in England for a number of important reasons some of which are mentioned below.

First there was the rejection of the authority of the Grand Lodge of London which, by proposing to control the activity of the Lodges through the setting up of certain rules on the basis of Anderson's Constitutions, had not managed to ensure the obedience and faithfulness of all English Lodges. Furthermore other Lodges, some distance from London, did not even know of its existence. So for different reasons, these Lodges were irregular. We can therefore suppose that they adopted rituals which in some ways were different from those imposed by the Grand Lodge of London. Some variants may have concerned the Royal Arch which was understood as a true ceremony and most authentic expression of ancient Freemasonry.

However, the most important reason for the development of the Royal Arch is perhaps to be found in its Christian content. In its first manifestations and for more than half a century thereafter, it had a decidedly Christian character. The Charges contained in the Ancient Manuscripts, familiar to operative masons since the 14th century, extended Christian feelings to speculative Freemasonry, feelings which found expression even in the 18th century in spite of what may be called the official de-Christianizing of the Craft by the Constitutions of Anderson in 1723. We can therefore suppose that, in the Lodges which recognised the authority of the Grand Lodge of London and in which the ceremony of the Royal Arch took place, the rituals were highly Christian in character. It may even be that the strenuous attempt to restore the Christian bases of operative Freemasonry was recognised in the Royal Arch. Whatever, the ritual of the Royal Arch expressed Christian contents throughout the whole of the 18th century. In the revision of 1835, which came about due to the need to bring the rituals of the Royal Arch into line with those of the Craft, most of these disappeared, though some have been preserved up to the present day.

One of the principal causes of dispute and conflict between Moderns and Antients was due to the different attitude that they adopted towards the Royal Arch. While the Antients adopted it and regarded it as a pillar of the masonic building, the Moderns officially ignored and opposed it, although they actually practised it.

Nevertheless, the Royal Arch spread more and more quickly, some important stages in its growth being marked by the constitution of the Grand Chapters. (The term 'chapter' has a specifically religious connotation and indicates the place in which the masons of the Royal Arch met; their meeting place was not therefore the Lodge).

The first Grand Chapter was constituted in 1766 by Lord Blayney, Grand Master of the Moderns who, together with the Most Excellent Companions (as the brothers of the Royal Arch were called) enacted the Constitutive Charter, known as the Charter of Compact, on the basis of which the Supreme Grand Royal Arch Chapter of England was formed and whose task it was to confer legitimacy on the existing Chapters as well as newly constituted ones.

The response of the Antients was not long in coming: five years later they constituted their own Grand Chapter though this did not become active until 1783.

Meanwhile the time was approaching for the re-unification of the Grand Lodges of the Moderns and the Antients and in their negotiations, the Royal Arch was a problem for which a satisfactory solution had to be found, otherwise all hope of reconciliation would have been lost. The Moderns declared that they were already disposed to accept its official recognition, for which the 1813 Act of Union declared and proclaimed that the 'Pure Ancient Freemasonry consists of three degrees, and no more: viz, those of the Entered Apprentice, the Fellow Craft and the Master Mason, including the Supreme Order of the Holy Royal Arch'. From that moment, the Freemasonry of the Royal Arch was officially recognised as the completion of the Third Degree.

Following the example of the unification of the two Grand Lodges, came the constitution in 1817 of the Supreme Grand Chapter of Royal Arch Masons of England, formed by the union of the two Grand Chapters, the Grand Chapter of Moderns in 1766 and the Grand Chapter of Antients in 1771.

The United Grand Lodge of England took note of the constitution of the Supreme Grand Chapter and on 3rd September in the same year approved the following resolution: 'That the Grand Lodge having been informed that the two Grand Chapters of the Order of the Royal Arch, existing prior to the Union of the Craft, had formed a junction and that the Laws and Regulations of that body had been, as far as possible, assimilated, to those of the Craft, it was Resolved Unanimously that the Grand Lodge will at all times be disposed to acknowledge the proceedings of the Grand Chapter, and so long as their arrangements do not interfere with the Regulations of the Grand Lodge, and are in conformity with the Act of Union, they will be ready to recognize, facilitate, and uphold the same'.

Clearly then, while the United Grand Lodge of England formally approved of the constitution of the Supreme Grand Chapter because it feared dispute, it had formulated a cautionary clause affirming that the 'arrangements' of the Royal Arch should not interfere with its Regulations and with the Act of Union.

The Royal Arch spread with some variations in Ireland, Scotland and America.

The three symbolic degrees of the Craft express the idea that the process of initiatic perfection is realised by reaching the degree of master mason. No other degree is required. Nevertheless it was not long before it was necessary to add other degrees to the basic symbolic ones. This may well have been because the emphasis on the speculative nature of Freemasonry made the procedure of initiatic perfection more complex and more greatly articulated. In any case, there is a line of continuity between the first three symbolic degrees constituting the Craft, and the Degrees constituting the Rite, or rather the Rites that are developed on the unique basis of the Craft. Among these, the most important and widespread is the Ancient and Accepted Scottish Rite. With regards to the nature, structure and functions of the Rite, I will limit myself to describing this Rite only.

The constitution of the High Degrees (or Rites) was attributed to Andrew Michael Ramsay, and dates back to around the middle of the eighteenth century. 'Ramsay's speech' is without doubt a fundamental document of modern Freemasonry. It is the speech he was to have given on 4th March 1737, as Grand Chaplain of the Grand Lodge of France. It is particularly important because it contains some ideas on the basis of which the Ancient and Accepted Scottish Rite was built. Ramsay was made a mason in a London Lodge, probably in 1728. He considered Freemasonry to be an association comprising all peoples and uniting all spirits and hearts in the same aim. He proposed it should become 'a great intellectual nation', and dreamt of transforming it into an academy of scholars and artists. He also proposed printing a universal dictionary of the sciences.

The first document destined to regulate the activity of the Ancient and Accepted Scottish Rite was given by the Constitutions and Regulations of 1762, edited by nine new members nominated by the Sovereign of the Sublime Grand

Council of the Sublime Princes of the Royal Secret of the Grand Orients of Paris and Berlin.

Ramsay's speech and the Regulations of 1762 prepared the way for the Grand Constitutions of 1786, which bore the name of Frederick II, King of Prussia. Charles Edward, last offspring of the Stuart family, was the head of both ancient and modern Freemasonry. He was appointed as Grand Master and his successor Frederick II accorded particular protection to Freemasonry. At that time the Rite of Perfection, from which the Ancient and Accepted Scottish Rite was to develop, was made up of 25 degrees, the last being that of Prince of the Royal Secret. Discussions on innovatory projects that took place in 1782 caused Frederick to fear that Freemasonry might become prey to the anarchy of those who could degrade it and bring about its destruction. Therefore he conceived the purpose of concentrating the sovereign masonic power with which he had been invested in a Council of Grand General Inspectors who, after his death, could regulate the governing of High Freemasonry in conformity with the Constitution and Statutes. On 1st May 1786, he increased to 33 degrees the hierarchy of the Ancient and Accepted Scottish Rite, which until then had been limited to 25. He named the 33rd degree the Powerful and Sovereign Grand Inspector General. The power attributed to this degree and destined to govern the Rite was concentrated in a Sovereign Chapter under the name and title of Supreme Council of Sovereign Grand Inspector Generals, 33rd and Last Degree of the Rite. Today all over the world, the Ancient and Accepted Scottish Rite has the order conferred by these Constitutions.

Many reasonable doubts exist as to whether the Regulations of 1762 and the Grand Constitutions of 1786 were authentic documents. Nevertheless, even if the Constitutions of 1786 were not signed by Frederick II in Berlin, they only too clearly reflect his personality and the cultural environment that surrounded him.

The Grand Constitutions of 1786 prepared the way for the first Supreme Council in the world. John Mitchell and Frederick Dalcho, both Deputy Grand Inspector Generals, set up at Charleston, South Carolina the Supreme Council which first opened on May 31st 1801. This Supreme Council sent out a circular in which it announced that its organization had been completed and proclaimed the Grand Constitutions of 1786 as the law of its existence and the origin of its powers.

The Ancient and Accepted Scottish Rite developed from the Bordeaux Rite of Perfection, as well as from the Paris Aristocratic Chapter of Clermont and the Council of Emperors of the East and West.

Albert Pike, in his important work *Morals and Dogma*, examined exhaustively the various Rituals of all degrees in the Scottish Rite.

The Charleston Supreme Council conferred upon de Grasse a Patent as Sovereign Grand Inspector General on February 21st 1802 and pronounced him Grand Commander of the Supreme Council of the French West Indian Islands, giving him the power to establish other Scottish Rite circles. On his return to France in 1804 he established the Supreme Council of France, in 1805 that of Italy, that of Spain in 1809 and of Belgium in 1817.

The principles of the Ancient and Accepted Scottish Rite were well expressed by Henry C. Clausen, Sovereign Grand Commander of the Supreme Council, 33 (Mother Supreme Council of the World) when he affirmeds in his very important book *Messages for a Mission* that 'We learn our mission in a system of progressive degrees of instruction. We teach our members the highest ethics, the wise expositions of philosophy and religion, the blessing of charity. Our code of personal conduct stems from the precepts of chivalry, the Ten Commandments and the Golden Rule. We reveal truly the wisdom of the Lesser and the Greater Mysteries and their symbols of words and phrases long considered lost. These were the truths that Plato, Pythagoras, Socrates, Homer and other intellects of the ages held in high esteem, that have reappeared in later religions, and that never were disclosed until after timely preparation and purification of selected and trusted initiates. Our degrees represent the study and reflections of many men...Our members therefore receive a gift of the greatest value. They gain a comprehensive knowledge of our heritage of history, philosophy, religion, morality, freedom and tolerance...These may well lead to self knowledge, clarity of mind and energy of will that propel toward personal success in life.. We stand for positive programs but fight with moral courage and enthusiasm every force or power that would seek to destroy freedom, including spiritual despostism and political tyranny.. Ours therefore has been a strong voice for human dignity, justice, morality and civic responsability'.

The Ancient and Accepted Scottish Rite can be depicted as a pyramid which has at its base three symbolic degrees from which are extended the fourth to the thirty-third degrees.

The degrees of the pyramid are as follows:

Symbolic degrees

1 Entered Apprentice
2 Fellow Craft
3 Master Mason (including the Holy Royal Arch)

Capitular degrees

4 Secret Master
5 Perfect Master
6 Intimate Secretary
7 Provost and Judge
8 Intendant of the Building
9 Elect of Nine
10 Elect of Fifteen
11 Sublime Elect
12 Grand Master Architect
13 Royal Arch of Solomon
14 Grand Elect Perfect
15 Knight of the East
16 Prince of Jerusalem
17 Knight of the East and West
18 Knight Rose-Croix
19 Grand Pontiff

Philosophical Degrees

20 Grand Master of Symbolic Lodges
21 Noachite or Prussian Knight
21 Knight of the Royal Axe
23 Chief of the Tabernacle
24 Prince of the Tabernacle
25 Knight of the Brazen Serpent
26 Prince of Mercy
27 Knight of the Temple
28 Knight of the Sun
29 Knight of St Andrew
30 Knight Kadosh

Administrative Degrees

31 Grand Inspector Inquisitor Commander
32 Sublime Prince of the Royal Secret
33 Sovereign Grand Inspector General

The advocates of the High Degrees maintain that the process of perfection beginning with initiation should be realised by the mason passing from one degree to the next up the scale until he reaches the highest, the 33rd degree. The notion of the 'rough stone' is taken up again. He who is initiated into Freemasonry is like a rough stone that must be smoothed. Smoothing consists of patient work within the Pillars of the Temple where the secrets of how to acquire new virtues are revealed. The mason who has given proof of having learnt the virtues of the degree to which he belongs (smoothing his rough stone) is proposed by the Lights of the Temple for a subsequent or higher degree. The aspiration of every Scottish Rite mason is to reach the apex of the pyramid, the 33rd degree. Very few manage to do so. The process of initiatic perfection, accomplished in the passing from one degree to the next immediately above it is cumulative, in the same way in which the smoothing of the rough stone is continuous. The mason who climbs all the degrees of the pyramid reaches perfection (the Sublime Secret is revealed to him).

So now we can draw our conclusions regarding the Constitutions and the significance of their possibly being modified. Radical changes in the Constitutions concerning the fundamental aspects characterising the hierarchical structure of the degrees of the Rite and the Craft, in the ritual forms concerning the initiatic secret and in the constituent elements of masonic philosophical anthropology are not possible since some essential pillar of masonic thought might be damaged or destroyed. Nevertheless, modification of the Constitutions is desirable where a discrepancy exists between the content that is formalised in them and the historical evolution of masonic thought that has since been codified in authoritative documents of the Grand Lodges. A clear example of this is the deistic content of the first and sixth Charges of Anderson, which are clearly in conflict with the position Freemasonry has adopted towards religious issues since the *Act of Union* of 1813. (This we will discuss more fully in Chapter 6 when we examine the relationship between Freemasonry and religion). Furthermore, we must remember that certain proscriptions or orders in the Constitutions are clearly linked to the historical, political and social context of the time in which they were written. Consequently, revision is not only legitimate but necessary.

Chapter 6

Freemasonry and Religion

Various points have emerged in the course of the preceding chapters on the relationship between Freemasonry and religions. Since they are particularly important both on a philosophical and practical level I feel they should be explained and developed further. To do so I would like first to examine a document recently approved by the United Grand Lodge of England (June 1st 1985) entitled *Freemasonry and Religion*) the text follows:

Introduction

Following recent comments made on Freemasonry and Religion and investigations carried out by several churches into the compatibility of Freemasonry with Christianity, the Board has decided to make public the following declaration, further to an original one which was approved by the Grand Lodge in September 1962 and confirmed in December 1981.

Basic Statement

Freemasonry is not a religion nor is it a substitute for religion. It demands of its members a belief in a Supreme Being but provides no system of faith of its own.

Freemasonry is open to men of all religious faiths. The discussion of religion at its meetings is forbidden.

The Supreme Being

The name used for the Supreme Being enable men of different faiths to join in prayer (to God as each sees Him) without the terms of the prayer causing dissension among them.

There is no separate Masonic God; a Freemason's God remains the God of the religion he professes.

Freemasons meet in common respect for the Supreme Being as He remains Supreme in their individual religions, and it is no part of Freemasonry to attempt to join religions together. There is therefore no composite Masonic God.

Volume of the Sacred Law

The Bible, referred to by Freemasons as the Volume of the Sacred Law, is always open at every Masonic meeting.

The Obligations of Freemasonry

The obligations taken by Freemasons are sworn on or involve the Volume of the Sacred Law, or the book held sacred by those concerned. They are undertakings to help keep secret a Freemason's means of recognition, and to follow the principles of Freemasonry.

The physical penalties which are purely symbolic do not form part of an Obligation. The commitment to follow the principles of Freemasonry is however deep.

Freemasonry Compared with Religion

Freemasonry lacks the basic elements of religion:

a) It has no theological doctrine, and by forbidding religious discussion at its meetings will not allow a Masonic theological doctrine to develop.

b) It offers no sacraments.

c) It does not claim to lead to salvation by works, by secret knowledge or by any other means. The secrets of Freemasonry are concerned with modes of recognition and not with salvation.

Freemasonry Supports Religion

Freemasonry is far from indifferent to religion. Without interfering in religious practice it expects each member to follow his own faith, and to place above all other duties his duty to God by whatever name He is known. Its moral teachings are acceptable to all religions.

Freemasonry is thus a supporter of religion.

The fundamental Declaration was issued by the United Grand Lodge of England, the highest masonic authority, endowed with the title of Mother Lodge of the World. This declaration therefore assumes the importance of a constuitive act, whereby it not only takes a stand in the face of any misunderstanding that might occur where the relationship between Freemasonry and religion undergoes analysis, but also functions as a basic document valid for all Jurisdictions recognised by the United Grand Lodge of England.

Therefore it is binding. It is for this reason that the document must be examined with the greatest attention.

Let us first consider the introduction. By referring to 'recent comments' and 'investigations carried out by several churches into the incompatibility of Freemasonry with Christianity', an underlying preoccupation can be identified. This preocupation concerns itself with the possibility that discussions on the relationship between Freemasonry and religion might alter and confuse the authentic principles of masonic tradition. This urged a fundamental declaration in which the point of view of the United Grand Lodge of England is precisely defined and stressed.

The document contains the following statements:

1 Freemasonry is not a religion, nor is it a substitute for religion.
2 It is no part of Freemasonry to attempt to join religions together.
3 There is therefore no composite Masonic God.
4 There is no separate Masonic God.
5 Masons meet in common respect for the Supreme Being.

These simple and essential affirmations are sufficient for an opinion to be formed on the three possible ways of viewing the relationship between Freemasonry and religion:

1 Freemasonry is a religion
2 Freemasonry is the *meeting-point* of several (possibly all) religions
3 Freemasonry is not a religion.

In the course of its history, Freemasonry has experienced all three ways of conceiving its relationship with religion

It began with Operative Freemasonry, accepting and sharing the belief in the God of a Christian religion. Subsequently, having taken inspiration from deism from the times of its origin, Speculative Freemasonry set about searching for a Universal Religion based on human reason (see Charges 1 and 6 in the previous chapter) with the obvious aim of preserving a religious foundation, albeit different from a specifically Christian one: thus the need for a meeting-point among some (or all) religions, where no conflict or misunderstanding can arise over this common and rational foundation. Yet it did not take long for the idea of a Universal Religion to appear Utopian. The search for a common foundation proved to be ridden with obstacles both on a practical and theoretical level. From these limitations and the issues that emerge, it becomes increasingly clear that Freemasonry must be explicitly distinguished from all forms of religion (particular or composite). Freemasonry, therefore, is not to be confused with anything that may act as a substitute for religion. This requirement, already laid down in the *Act of Union* of 1813, is taken up again in the fundamental declaration we are examining in such a way as to remove any shadow of doubt.

These same concepts are corroborated in the document of the Grand Lodge, under the specification that the mason is required to believe in a Supreme Being but with no system of faith being indicated. Belief in the 'Supreme Being' is, therefore, a notion that is in no way representative of the god of a particular religion, or a composite god originating from a common point of reference shared by particular religions, or the god of any surrogate religion. Indeed, the Board of the Grand Lodge maintains that belonging to Freemasonry and professing a religious faith are not incompatible. It claims that 'Freemasonry is open to men of all religious faiths', that 'a Freemason's God remains the

God of the religion he professes' and that 'it (Freemasonry) expects each member to follow his own faith and to place above all other duties his duty to God by whatever name He is known'. One cannot help pointing out that in the western world, the principal declared case of incompatibility between Freemasonry and religion was by the Roman Catholic Church, but this was a one-sided decision of the Catholic Church itself. For its own part, even if historically speaking it has had to pay for the consequences of this declared incompatibility, Freemasonry has always been willing to welcome into its Temples men professing a religious faith, as long as they are disposed to accept a Supreme Being 'as he remains Supreme in their individual religions'. That is, in Freemasonry there can exist both men who have different religious beliefs (they are committed to a God in all the names with which he is known) and men who have do not adhere to any specific religious belief. The only condition is that both must believe in a Supreme Being—the governing principle—and at the same time in the aim and justification of the initiatic process which sets the mason on the road to betterment. The common characteristic is reflected in the Supreme Being, who represents the *minimal condition* for belonging to Freemasonry without excluding however the fact that this Supreme Being may coincide with the divinity of the specific religious faith that a mason professes.

The presence in Freemasonry of men with very different attitudes towards particular religions caused a cautionary clause to be added, according to which 'the discussion of religion at its meetings is forbidden'. But the Declaration pronounced by the Board goes much further with a statement to the effect that 'Freemasonry, by forbidding religious discussion at its meetings will not allow a Masonic theological doctrine to develop'. This assertion is very important and goes way beyond the vetoing of religious or political discussions imposed by the Constitutions of Anderson. It expounds the danger of some form of dogma being created on some point of agreement if religion were to be discussed. Cases of this kind are anything but improbable. As we have seen in the previous chapter, they appear clearly from the contents of the Landmarks concerning the theme of religion in many Grand Lodges. Intervention from the Board is then highly significant since it re-affirms the principle of tolerance, which is at the heart of masonic thinking, where the mason (as such) may not form any kind of religious dogma, even if a general agreement has been reached. Furthermore, one cannot help noticing in this veto, an attempt to avoid a rebirth of deism in any new form.

This open disposition of Freemasonry towards individual religions is further confirmed by the stand the Grand Lodge takes on the Book of the Sacred Law. 'The Bible, referred to by Freemasons as the Volume of the Sacred Law, is always open at every Masonic meeting'. This statement tends to emphasise the close connection between Freemasonry and religion, not in the sense of masons being slaves to religion but rather as an act of due respect towards it. It is certainly wrong to see any stronger commitment in this declaration. In fact the book is simply left open and not assimilated through the reading of passages. To confirm this, the following specification is made, that 'the obligations taken by Freemasons are sworn on or involve the Volume of the Sacred Law, *or the book held sacred by those concerned*' (my italics). Tolerance of masons towards all religions is again emphasised.

The document of the Grand Lodge then goes on to discuss the question of swearing oaths (of the initiatic secret) and comparing Freemasonry and religious practice.

As far as the oath and the secret are concerned, the assertion is that 'the obligations taken by Freemasons are sworn on or involve the Volume of the Sacred Law' and that such oaths are intended in order 'to held keep secret a Freemason's means of recognition, and follow the principles of Freemasonry'. Such propositions are made to emphasise the importance of the oath, reflected in the principles of Freemasonry which all must follow.

As I have shown in the previous chapters, the oath constitutes a solemn act, characterising the moment of initiation and ascendence to higher levels by means of which the masonic ethical dimension is conferred. What is more, the oath concerns the initiatic secret. And it is through the initiatic secret that a first essential difference between Freemasonry and religious practice comes to light. The Board of the Grand Lodge explicitly declares that 'the secrets of Freemasonry are concerned with modes of recognition and not with salvation'; this means that all those who try to see in the initiatic secret the source of man's salvation are wrong. The notion of 'salvation' is totally alien to masonic thought. And it is not only because masonic thinking does not contemplate any form of dogma and theology, that there is no room for any analagous form of sacramental practice in the initiation of the mason. Freemasonry 'offers no sacraments'. In fact since the sacrament is an effective sign of divine grace, the practice of sacraments presupposes on the one hand actual *intervention* by God in the life of man, and on the other that man is the object of such redemptive intervention. Since masonic thinking *as such* is alien both to the idea of a personal and provident God and to the idea of man's salvation, the administration of the sacraments has no meaning for it whatsoever.

Yet this does not mean that Freemasonry is hostile to religion and its practices. The document of the Grand Lodge concludes with an explicit declaration, 'Freemasonry supports religion'. Far from being indifferent to religion 'it expects each member to follow his own faith'.

Finally the assertion that 'Its (Freemasonry's) moral teachings are acceptable to all religions' is particularly important. This stresses the principle that Freemasonry is not opposed to religion but it considers it essential to the development of man, without being confused with it. Specifically the affirmation that the moral principles with which Freemasonry is infused may be accepted by all religions is extremely important, since it clearly declares, at least on a moral plane, that there can be no conflict between Freemasonry and religion.

The picture the document of the United Grand Lodge of England offers on the relationship between Freemasonry and religion is unequivocal. Even the assertions made at various levels are specific and leave no room for any reasonable doubt as to how they are to be interpreted. However, in pronouncing this document, the Board of the Grand Lodge does not intend to present a complete philosophical view of the question. They limit themselves to proclaiming some basic principles without discussing whether they were justified or founded. In the pages to follow, I intend to return to the theoretical framework of philosophical foundation taking as my starting point the propositions enclosed in the document.

The propositions we have analysed in the document can be divided into three categories:

a) propositions on the nature of T.G.A.O.T.U.
b) propositions on the compatibility between the ethics of Freemasonry and the ethics of particular religions, and
c) propositions on religious practices.

Let us take them in order. As far as point a) is concerned,

the position of the Grand Lodge can be summarised in four fundamental statements':

1 Freemasonry is not a religion
2 Freemasonry is not an expression of a theological syncretism (there is no masonic God)
3 Masons have in common a respect for the Supreme Being
4 Freemasonry is open to men of all beliefs.

So the thesis that I propose to maintain is that for all four statements to hold fast the T.G.A.O.T.U. must be understood as a *regulative ideal in a non-exclusive sense.* For the sake of simplicity, I will call this thesis 'non-exclusive regulativism'. Therefore non-exclusive regulativism is seen to be a distinguishing feature in the masonic conception of T.G.A.O.T.U.

Let us return to the deistic phase of speculative Freemasonry. In this phase, T.G.A.O.T.U. was understood as a meeting-point of the theological components of particular religions. In other words understood as a god who expresses the *minimal* contents (within the confines of pure human rationality) of the beliefs of all men. For this reason, he cannot be for instance, a provident or personal god, since providence and personality are not characteristics that all men (or all religions) are disposed to concede to the Supreme Being. So generally speaking the masonic deistic god cannot possess all the properties that each single religious conception attributes to him. Now we must ask ourselves whether a mason can be coherent if he accepts a deistic god declaring at the same time that he believes in a personal and provident Christian God. The answer is clearly no, since the deistic god is accepted in his ontological reality just as the Christian God is and therefore it is impossible to maintain that the Supreme Being is provident and at the same time is not provident.

Apart from the fact that the crisis in philosophical deism necessarily caused masonic thinking to falter, by forcing it to accept a substantial basic theism (theism issuing in a radical immanentism of both the ontological and axiological kind), the deistic interpretation of T.G.A.O.T.U. is in any case incompatible with the principle of tolerance expressed in the preceding statement 4. Besides, a deistic position is clearly incompatible with statements 1 and 2. In fact if we were able to accept the deistic meaning of T.G.A.O.T.U. Freemasonry would make its own idea of a specific masonic god by transforming itself into a particular religion. As we have already intimated in the previous chapters, the difficulties contained within the deistic conception of the Supreme Being can be overcome by accepting the interpretation that he is a regulative ideal. It is not a question here of repeating the considerations we have already made. Rather it is a matter of presenting the motive for which the conception of T.G.A.O.T.U. as a regulative ideal is a necessary premise in order to prove the above four statements satisfactory. To conceive the Supreme Being as a regulative ideal means seeing the Supreme Being as a principle capable of giving sense and validity to the moral tension in man: a principle that reflects the perfection to which man in his moral actions continuously aspires. One may ask whether the simple acceptance of the Supreme Being as a regulative ideal (without any further specification) already excludes the fact that this Supreme Being may be further interpreted as the god of some particular religion (and so endowed with an ontological reality). I think the exclusion is only possible if we add the adverbial specification 'purely' to the term 'regulative', allowing T.G.A.O.T.U. to be understood in an *exclusively* regulative sense. In which case we mean that T.G.A.O.T.U. does not *in actual fact* exist as a separate deity, even if his regulative function towards transcendence with respect to man holds fast. Naturally a mason can accept this rigorously lay point of view and in this sense he will not be able coherently to share any religious faith in which the real existence of a transcendent god is an essential requirement. But this is not the position of the mason as such. To assert this means accepting the position as the official position of Freemasonry from a *purely* regulative point of view, which would anyway exclude the concept of the regulative ideal from being able to be *integrated* with some stronger meaning of divinity. That this cannot be the official position of Freemasonry is immediately clear from the way it opposes the preceding conclusion with statement 4. Secondly, by assuming an exclusivist point of view, Freemasonry is again committed to being a religion (of the obviously natural type), given that, however much it denies the true existence of God, it must nevertheless propose its own image of God (as a purely regulative ideal) distinct from and in contrast to those of other religions. And this goes against clause 1.

This is why I have spoken of non-exclusive regulativism. Now we must give some definitive specification as to what I intend to propose with this term. Freemasonry places T.G.A.O.T.U., understood as a regulative ideal, as a minimal condition for every mason but it does *not* conceive him in a way that *excludes* the fact that masons, *as individual men* can attribute to him the *characteristics* and *valences* which the various religions confer upon divinity. Here we are not speaking of a *purely* regulative ideal but simply of a regulative ideal. So then alongside the minimal condition of believing in the Supreme Being as a regulative ideal, posed as a *necessary condition in order to belong to* Freemasonry, we need the condition that individual faiths are not to be excluded. The *minimum* asked of a Mason is that he believes in a regulative ideal. *This does not* however *exclude* the fact that the regulative ideal in which a mason believes may refer to the same god in which the mason believes not as a mason but, for example, as a Christian. In this case, the condition of the regulative ideal remains the same, even if it is absorbed into the stronger condition of belief in the god of one's religious faith.

It seems to me that this conception of T.G.A.O.T.U. ensures that all four statements summarising the thought of the Grand Lodge on the nature of T.G.A.O.T.U. can be considered satisfactory. Above all it is evident that Freemasonry is not a religion. It is in fact typical of every religion to hypothesise the existence of a divinity; but Freemasonry only requires as a minimal condition, acceptance of the regulative valence of the Supreme Being. Secondly, since a regulative ideal does not have to be *determined in all its aspects*, Freemasonry is not obliged as in the case of deism, to accept a position of theological syncretism, thus avoiding the creation of a masonic god. Yet among the conditions necessary for belonging to Freemasonry, masons are required to believe in the Supreme Being, at least as a regulative principle. It follows that each mason has a respect for the Supreme Being in common with all others. Then, on the strength of the condition of non-exclusion, Freemasonry can declare itself open to men of all religious faiths. In short a position such as non-exclusive regulativism offers the great advantage of accepting true tolerance which cannot be guaranteed by positions such as deism.

Some important consequences emerge from the conclusions drawn so far. First we must note the distinction between Freemasonry understood as a *concept* and Freemasonry understood as a *society of men*. We may say that:

a) *Freemasonry as a concept* is equivalent to 'non-exclusive regulativism'
(b) *Freemasonry as a society of men* is equivalent to 'non-exclusivist masons who accept only the regulative point of view (*regulativist* masons) and religious non-exclusive regulativist masons (*religious* masons)'

(a) means that the concept of Freemasonry is defined by non-exclusive regulativism, that is by the minimum requirement necessary to belong to the Freemasonry. b) means that Freemasonry understood as a society of men, can be divided into two sub-groups: one of *regulativist masons* who share the regulative point of view and the other of *religious masons* who integrate the regulative point of view with the faith of some particular religion.

From definitions a) and b) we have the following consequences.

Consequence 1: If, in the presence of at least one religious mason, regulativist masons were to claim that Freemasonry should be purely regulative (i.e. excluding the possibility of adding any religious faith to the minimum requirement) and thus becoming exclusive regulativist, then a form of *integralism* would be created, and the principle of tolerance denied which by its very definition, is the negation of all forms of integralism.

Consequence 2: If, in the presence of at least one regulativist mason, religious masons were to claim that Freemasonry should be a religion, then a form of integralism would be created and the principle of tolerance violated.

Consequence 3: By avoiding the creation of any form of integralism, the principle of tolerance regulates the authentic relationship between regulativist and religious masons.

To conclude, the thesis of non-exclusive regulativism is the philosophical justification for two propositions ('Freemasonry *is not* a religion'and 'he individual mason *may have* a religious faith' which in all appearance seem to be contradictory but which in fact express the truest and most authentic foundation of masonic thought.

If non-exclusive regulativism guarantees compatibility between Freemasonry and particular individual religions as regards the existence of God, the problem of their compatibility arises from an ethical point of view. And so we come to discuss the propositions (included in point b) in the document concerning the statement that "the moral principles of Freemasonry can be accepted by all religions". How is it possible to make a declaration of this generality and importance? It is clear in fact that various principles of an ethical nature are derived both from the regulative ideal and the principles of various religions. How is it possible to guarantee that there will be no conflicting issues between them? The first step to be taken in this direction consists in determining where masonic ethical principles stand in relation to principles of religious ascendancy. There are two hypotheses here. According to the first, masonic ethical principles concern man as man and consequently they express a masonic anthropology as an *alternative* to all others. Since every religion proposes a global image of man (what suits man as such), and presents ethical obligation to be referred to man as such, this leads to an incompatibility between Freemasonry and religion on an ethical plane. In fact, both Freemasonry and religion would claim the right to provide the just scale of ethical prescriptions, and conflict could be avoided only on condition that between religion and Freemasonry there were a substantial identity, against the theory of non-exclusive regulativism. On the other hand, the hypothesis at stake here is already in itself incompatible with the regulativism we have determined. How is it possible for the same individual to share the same ethical principles when he belongs to that religion and is at the same time a mason, unless religion and masonic anthropology coincide? But earlier on, we maintained that Freemasonry cannot be a religion. So ethical Freemasonry cannot reflect the ethics of a man as such.

The conclusion that we have reached is already indicative of the second hypothesis we can use to define the relationship between masonic ethics and ethics of religion. As we have already mentioned, religions propose a global image of man, and consequently, give rise to a form of general ethics concerning human duties as a whole. Unless mistaken for a religious kind of ethics, masonic ethics reflects that part of general ethics concerning *the action of the mason as such.* This hypothesis is the logical consequence of the difficulties met with above, but for the purpose of practicality, a fundamental presupposition is required: it is necessary to be able to define the specific of the *masonic action.* Strange as it might seem, in order to determine a compatibility between the ethical principles of Freemasonry and the ethics of religion, one has to resort to finding a definition of masonic action. Yet this strangeness will vanish when we consider the fact that, if masonic principles are to be understood as principles belonging to a chapter on general ethics, then some criteria of attribution must be provided. What do these criteria depend on if not on the very criteria of masonic action? We have only to think of the concept of social ethics' social ethics is that part of ethics which concerns the principles that serve as a guide for the *social action* of man. Just as the definition of social ethics presupposes that of social action, so does the definition of masonic ethics presuppose that of masonic action. The two cases are perfectly parallel. So, it should be reasonably clear that masonic actions are those actions of the mason aimed at making him reach *perfection as a mason.* That is they are remarkable in respect to rituality and in view of the masonic regulative ideal. In this way, we can justify the assertion that there are specific ethical principles concerning the actions of the mason as such. Do these principles agree with ethical principles *tout court*?

No, they do not, because on the grounds of the hypothesis of non-exclusive regulativism, the mason *may* be a believer, and in which case he will have ethical obligations regarding actions that are not notable from a masonic point of view, but that are, on the contrary, essential (for example, attitude towards prayer, etc) for his religious conception. Only where a mason believes exclusively in the purely regulative ideal will masonic anthropology (the complex of propositions characterising the image of the masonic man) become anthropology *tout court*; in the other case, masonic anthropology remains a 'pass card' to the 'mosaic' of global anthropology.

If the second hypothesis guarantees the possibility of questioning an ethical coherence between religions and Freemasonry, they can be excluded *a priori* from the particular cases of incompatibility. In order to exclude these too, we must compare the plan of ethical perfection as proposed by Freemasonry to the ethical plan of the particular individual religions. Let us confine ourselves to some examples for an idea of the general outline such a comparison takes. We must ask ourselves, for instance, whether masonic perfection is compatible with Christian perfection or not. To be able to reply, we must immediately make a distinction; if the subject revolves round the concept of masonic perfection, the answer is surely no. This is a consequence of the considerations made earlier about the fact that masonic ethics is a chapter out of general ethics. If, on the other hand, by masonic perfection we also mean the process of *practical realisation* of this perfection, then the answer is decidedly more difficult. Let us consider, for example, the modalities of co-optation of the mason. It is common knowledge that the mason must accept the authority of the co-optant before coming to know the initiatic secret. The initiatic secret is not disclosed before entering Freemasonry and cannot be examined by the person who wishes to adhere to Freemasonry before he has stepped inside the circle of its associates. Is this prejudicial to a person's autonomy, which is the fundamental principle in the ethical theory of the Christian? It is not easy to give a straight answer. If keeping secret the contents of initiation were the fruit of an unjustified will, (on the part of the co-optant) tending to bind the will of the other, then there would surely be a lack of respect for a person's autonomy. But if secrecy is necessarily bound to the nature of the contents of the secret (which can only be revealed in a state of previous submission to the authority of the co-optant), then incompatibility vanishes. It cannot be denied that the opposite has occurred during the course of history but this cannot be put down to the initiatic secret.

We have yet to discuss the problem of the meaning of religious practices in relation to those connected to masonic ritual (proposition c). Given the central position of Christian religious practice in the document of the United Grand Lodge of England, I will try to deal with the issue in the pages to follow, where we will discuss not only practices but the whole context of Christian anthropology in relation to its masonic counterpart. In any case, it would not be possible to discuss the former adequately without extending the comparison to the whole of anthropology.

The above-mentioned document gives the explicit assertion from the Grand Lodge that Freemasonry does not offer its associates any type of ritual comparable to the Christian sacraments or seeking the salvation of man. This should not sound strange in the light of the considerations developed above, as far as the meaning of masonic anthropology is concerned in respect to the anthropology of a religion. Masonic anthropology concerns only those aspects of man which make him a mason, whereas a religiously inspired anthropology provides a global image of man. For this reason, it is neither possible nor justified that a doctrine of the salvation of man should follow on from masonic anthropology, and not even an ordered practice for salvation such as exists in the sacraments. There is at most a doctrine associated with masonic thought, complete with a precise ritual, concerning the way in which man may better himself in an ethical attempt to reach the regulative ideal represented by the Supreme Being, but there is missing within it a doctrine on the origin of man and on his ultimate aim in life. The insistence with which Freemasonry asserts, after a history marked with different phases of thought, that it is not its intention to offer any specific religious teaching to man and that it is indeed open to all forms of faith, means that its anthropology is not an anthropology *tout court* and that it cannot satisfy all the questions of sense that each individual asks himself. As we have already said, it is possible for a mason to be content to accept only the sense that masonic teaching gives his life. This is the case of one who considers the ideal of the Supreme Being in a purely regulative sense, but he should start from the conviction that man does not need to be saved and consequently that he should not expect from Freemasonry any sacramental type of practice predisposed for his salvation. And Freemasonry does not oblige its associates to take this point of view; on the contrary, they are free to share the message of salvation of any religion as long as they distinguish between what belongs to Freemasonry and what is alien to it even though it may well be compatible.

The particular relationship between Freemasonry and religion stands out quite clearly if one attempts to make a direct comparison between the fundamental notions of masonic anthropology and, for example, the essential elements of Christian anthropology. As we have already seen, masonic anthropology can be linked to the five notions of the quintuple *Freedom, Tolerance, Brotherhood, Transcendence,*

Initiatic Secret. I think that Christian anthropology can be recognised in the following triple—*Freedom, Transcendence* (in the ontological sense), *Salvation*. Usually, the number of concepts is of little significance. But here it seems to me that the presence in Christian anthropology of only three elements is highly significant. In fact by considering the qualitative nature of masonic concepts it is easy to perceive that it is a question of concepts that are exclusively functional to the ethical life of man; the same concept of transcendence, in the sense that it converges with the regulative ideal, is seen as the centre of inspiration for ethical life; and even the initiatic secret is essentially ordered to the process of the ethical perfection of the mason. On the other hand, everything functions in accordance with the salvation of man, freedom is understood as having the capacity to decide for or against the offer of salvation that God makes to man, whereas salvation is the releasing of man from all forms of ill and the fruit of the intervention of the Christian God (transcendent, real and personal) in the history of man.

Given the central position of the concept of salvation in Christian anthropology, one may wonder whether religion lacks the all important ethical dimension in the masonic conception of life. The answer is decidedly no, since the ethical principles are a natural consequence of the plan of salvation that God proposes to man. Man can be saved without any ethical commitment; but ethical commitment alone is not enough: what is needed is the determining help of God through His grace. This is where the function of the sacraments comes in, as effective signs of divine grace. It is evident then, that Christian anthropology is comprehensive, on a level of fundamental or derived notions, of all the aspects concerning man as such. Consequently, it is only logical that there should be a formal difference between the masonic quintuple and the Christian triple. Since the contents of the latter is more comprehensive, and the masonic quintuple may be limited to a context of a pure ethical consideration of man, the ethical counterpart of Christian anthropology will be codified in derived notions and not in those belonging to the original triple. On the other hand the ethical notions of masonic anthropology will all be fundamental, which is why they all appear in the original quintuple.

We may conclude, then, that in masonic conception, the Supreme Being must be understood at least as a symbolic expression of the masonic axiological ideal (regulative function of T.G.A.O.T.U.). For this, from a masonic point of view, it is not essential to distinguish between the ideal of perfection in man and transcendence. This distinction is, however, essential in the Christian conception where God is the foundation of the possibility of man being saved (his greatest perfection of realisation) but, at the same time, it is distinct from this state of perfection. This is justified by the fact that, for the Christian, God has an effective *personal reality*; it is He who proposes to man his plan of salvation and it is up to man to accept or reject it. On the other hand, this is not given in the masonic conception of the transcendent where a personal relationship is not required.

The consequences are notable. Personal intimacy with God (through prayer, etc) is particularly significant to the Christian, but not essential to the mason who may only see a regulative ideal in T.G.A.O.T.U., to which his own ethical activity must conform. The practising of the sacraments is just as significant to the Christian, in that they are effective signs of Grace in which the real intervention of God in the history of man is expressed. But this is not true for masonic ritual which holds an exclusive function within the project of masonic moral perfection (of a purely human nature) and which man alone proposes to himself. The idea of masonic perfection is necessarily linked only to an ideal of betterment in man from an essentially ethical point of view (without ethical betterment, one cannot attain social or political improvement either), and limited only to the field of human possibilities. For this reason, the idea of Christian perfection does not match masonic perfection, it is different in the sense that it includes values that are not exclusively ethical. This it seems to me is the principle reason why one speaks of salvation and not simply of the perfection of man.

The conclusion that we have reached is already indicative of the way in which the masonic Rituals are to be conceived. Indeed, the initiatic foundation of Freemasonry, represented by the fifth element of its anthropological quintuple, finds its deepest expression in the Rituals. If, for Freemasonry, initiation is the means by which to realise the ethical betterment of man, the Ritual is the tool on whose basis this ethical betterment is carried out gradually and continually. The Ritual teaches how to 'smooth the rough stone' and is therefore of fundamental importance. Nevertheless the Rituals have always been a source of misunderstanding and ambiguity. One reason for this possibly lies in the difficulty of relating the Rituals to masonic anthropology—the image of man according to Freemasonry. In fact, the Rituals *must* be above all the symbolic and allegorical expression of masonic anthropology.

The first and fundamental question to be asked is the following: should the Ritual be the expression of Freemasonry as a concept, as a society of men? Earlier on we saw that these two notions do not coincide and that a choice must be made in favour of one or the other. From our discussion so far, I think there can be only one answer: the Rituals should express the *minimum requirement* of Freemasonry, as reflected in non-exclusive regulativism (Freemasonry as a concept), in that it is the *common* foundation for all masons (if a mason rejects the minimum requirement then he is no longer a mason). Vice-versa, the Rituals cannot be an expression of 'something more' in respect to the common foundation. In fact if Christian masons were to expect the Rituals to include some specific contents of their religion, they would be forcing regulativist masons and other religious masons (Jews, Muslims, etc) to pursue initiatic perfection on the basis of elements they consider extraneous, thus violating the key foundation on which the masonic building rests, i.e. tolerance. This does not mean that the individual mason may not integrate the minimum foundation with the religious faith he professes, but the contents of this faith must not become part of the Rituals, since the Rituals *must be valid for all masons*. There is nothing to prevent a religious mason from adding elements expressing his own religious faith (prayer, invocation, etc) to the Rituals shared by all masons, but he *cannot expect* them to be accepted by all his fellow masons and be valid as a general characteristic of Freemasonry. His right to do so should not be confused with the concept of Freemasonry which does recognise this right, but does not make it compulsory for all masons. In conclusion, non-exclusive regulativism defines where the Rituals should be characterised. A fundamental consequence of this is that no reference should be made in the Rituals to the typical contents of religions, such as omnipotence, grace, salvation, faith, and so on. If these prescriptions are violated, religious contents are then introduced into the Rituals, which in particular circumstances, may cause profound contradictions to arise.

In Chapter 5, I outlined the origins and developments of the Royal Arch, showing that it is *officially* the completion of the Third Degree as seen in the 1813 Act of Union and that *it cannot oppose* the Regulations of the United Grand Lodge of England.

Here, I propose to compare the essential characteristics of the Royal Arch with the Declaration on Freemasonry and religion which we discussed in detail in this chapter.

We saw that in the early years of its development and for more than half a century the Royal Arch was based on Christian contents. Even after the ritual was revised in 1835 there were still elements of the Christian religion left. The question now is: do the Christian contents that are still present in the Royal Arch have a purely symbolic meaning or are they expressions of its real Christian nature? There are two possible answers: a) the Royal Arch *is not* a religion (neither Christian, Jewish nor any other) and b) the Royal Arch *is* a religion (Christian). Let us examine the consequences of the two possible answers.

If the Royal Arch is not a religion, then are its legends, taken from the Old and New Testament and integrated with alchemical metaphors, to be understood as simple symbolic expressions to be added to the legends of the Craft, and integrated with them in a coherent and unitary manner? The Christian references, therefore, lose their specificity and take on a wider sense so as to include even the typical meanings of other religions and to admit a simply regulative interpretation as explained in this same chapter.

Since it is the completion of the Third Degree (which in itself is the completion of the Second and First) the Royal Arch must preserve what it holds of the universality of Freemasonry, which was made possible by actually denying a religious foundation, thus being able to admit into the Lodges men professing different religious faiths as well as those who do not follow any specific religious dogma.

As far as the degrees of the Craft are concerned, Freemasonry is mainly understood as a society of men on the basis of its two possible definitions: actual men living in history and united in a community having the aim of perfecting themselves, and humanity according to the highest initiatic and moral principles inspired by transcendence (the Grand Architect of the Universe). The completion of the Third Degree through the Royal Arch should therefore be understood as emphasising the spiritual dimension of man by preserving the requisite of universality, which can only be realised if the Royal Arch is not an expression of a single religion (the Christian religion in particular).

If the Royal Arch is interpreted as a Christian religion difficulties and contradictions arise. Above all it becomes the negation of universality and therefore of tolerance, brotherhood and love among all men. Furthermore, the Royal Arch cannot be considered a closer study and completion of the Third Degree but 'something different'. The awareness of these problems resulted in changes being adopted in order to 'de-Christianise' the rituals in order to make them more acceptable to masons of all faiths.

If the Royal Arch were as a Christian religion, it could provoke a negative and restrictive judgement of the first three degrees of Freemasonry. Being principally a society of men in the sense I have explained, Freemasonry in its first three degrees could then be interpreteted as being *too human* due to the fact that it was that much further away from God, the true principle of Freemasonry. Anyone supporting this position might run the risk of integralism and intolerance. Feeling they possessed the truth, they would be only too ready to condemn and excommunicate those masons who did not share their 'authentic' conception of Freemasonry: or they might assume an attitude of superior benevolence in relation to those masons who, because of their conviction that the truth in Freemasonry is an incessant and gradual search and not a dogma revealed directly by God, did not want to rise to their level.

We have only to think of the difficulties in which the mason would find himself when, having learnt in the first three degrees that Freemasonry is not a religion, he were to 'discover', after entering the Royal Arch, that the true nature of Freemasonry was Christian. He might fall into a state of disillusionment, since he would have to admit that Freemasonry is not a religion (when he works in the Lodge) and that Freemasonry is a religion (when he works in the Chapter). Since man tends to remove the conflictual state by eliminating one of the terms of conflict, the mason who found find himself in this state of disillusionment would be forced to choose between the two possible solutions: renounce the Royal Arch, or re-interpret the first three degrees by extending to them the contents of Christianity. If he were not able to make this choice, the conflict would force him to examine his conscience and the possibility of rejecting Freemasonry would arise. The difficulties he would meet with on a personal and subjective plane can be projected onto an abstract and objective level, where the contradiction becomes irreconcilability between the two different positions. The conclusion is that, at least as regards the Craft, Freemasonry is or is not a religion It is not possible that at first it is not and then later it becomes one. Anyone wishing to support this viewpoint would find it remarkably difficult to justify.

From a legal point of view, a Christian interpretation of the Royal Arch would violate both the cautionary clause of 1817 and the 1985 Declaration on Freemasonry and Religion.

The philosophical thesis of non-exclusive regulativism, having denied the Royal Arch a Christian foundation, recognises in each individual mason of the Royal Arch the right to integrate the minimal requisite with the faith of his own religion, Christian, Jewish, Islamic or any other kind. In this way, it reaffirms the truly universal nature of Freemasonry.

Chapter 7

Freemasonry, Positivism and Science

It has emerged from our analysis in the previous chapter on the relationship between Freemasonry and religion, that there was an underlying concern on the part of the United Grand Lodge of England that within certain masonic circles, Freemasonry was believed to have a basic religious component. To avoid any misunderstanding it was stressed in the Declaration we have examined that Freemasonry is not a religion. Yet within masonic thought there is another tendency (or temptation), diametrically opposed to the religious tendency concerning positivism. Whereas with the former, the aim is to attempt to strengthen the ontological potency of T.G.A.O.T.U., the latter is directed at weakening him so radically that he is finally denied. The positivist tendency, therefore seen as the re-affirmation of a radically immanent concept would in its most extreme form, would lead to atheism. This positivist tendency has influenced masonic thinking in the past and as, for example, in the case of the Grand Orient of France, continues to do so. In fact influential positivists from Littré to Haeckel were masons and, as such, carried out at times a determining role in the basic choices characterising important decisions in some national Grand Orients. We need go no further than think of the influence Littré exerted on the decision taken by the Grand Orient of France to abolish the formula of The Great Architect of the Universe. Again, we have only to think in

Italy of the role Ausonio Franchi played in Italian Freemasonry through the Symbolic Rite. For these reasons alone it is important to review the principles of positivism in order to establish whether, and how far, it is compatible with masonic thought.

Positivism is understood here as a conceptual category and not in its historical development. Therefore the reflections that follow refer both to the positivism of Comte and Spencer as well as to logical positivism.

The term 'positivism' was coined by Saint Simon, and then used and imposed by Comte; it indicates a philosophical trend that was very popular in the second half of the nineteenth century and was manifested in various ways, from the 'social positivism' of Saint Simon and Comte to the evolutionistic positivism of Spencer, and to the philosophy of John Stuart Mill. It also created a cultural atmosphere that was extremely favourable towards scientific problems and methods and encouraged, more or less directly, the setting up of new scientific disciplines such as psychology and sociology.

In order to understand the general characteristics of positivism, we should first of all explain how it stands in respect to the cognitive capacity of human reason and the validity of certain instruments of knowledge. Positivism thus represents a certain philosophical attitude with respect to human knowledge. Generally speaking, it indicates which elements implicit in affirmations concerning the world, deserve to be called knowledge. Consequently, it distinguishes between which philosophical and scientific controversies are worth developing and examining more closely and which issues outside these limits are not worth considering. On these grounds, positivists distinguish between what can be rationally discussed and what cannot. This is expressed by the principle according to which human knowledge is substantially limited to a pure empirical base: any genuine idea is derived from experience, thus every supposition made regarding hidden existences, of which the empirical forms of existence would only be manifestations, is completely unfounded. The external world is independent of the knowledgeable subject. No knowledge excluding experience is given *a priori*. It is therefore the task of science to be familiar with the invarying laws of the external world. Language is the neutral expression of these laws. Having made a distinction between facts and values, science is concerned with the former, while values fall within the realm of subjectivity (expression of rules, reasons, ends, intentions, etc.) the existence of which is only accepted as far as it can be reduced to an observable datum. Sense converges with a sense of the verifiable. No sense exists outside what is empirically verifiable: to accept a sense beyond this point would mean crossing the bridge from science to metaphysics. The researcher is none other than the faithful transcriber of what is given in reality.

These epistemological assumptions show that there must be a fundamental unity in the methods of knowledge. In fact, positivism claims that methods of investigation into knowledge, valid for all aspects of experience, are identical. This methodological unity omits any consideration of the typical and specific characteristics of the single sciences which, therefore, prove insignificant. Positivists maintain that the most advanced natural sciences, and mathematical physics in particular, represent the highest level of scientific development and consequently become a criterion by which the other sciences must be measured to determine their level of maturity. It is from this comparison that, either because of an imprecision of the object or because of a lack of rigorous techniques of investigation, the human and social sciences, e.g. sociology, psychology, economics, history and the like, prove to be in an almost pre-scientific stage, far from the state of perfection of the exact natural sciences. This conviction leads to the desire for an even greater use in the human and social sciences of instruments that have already been experimentally validated in other sectors of scientific investigation. What I mean is, the sciences of nature become the methodological model for the development of human and social sciences. However, positivism goes beyond this declaration and expresses the hope that further progress may lead to a gradual elimination of the differences between the single sciences, until they are reduced to just one. It has often been claimed that physics will become this one science, since it has developed the most rigorous method of investigation. Thus, a general hypothesis is formulated of the reduction of all human knowledge to physical properties, of the translation of all scientific theories into statements regarding physical relations found in nature, and of the possibility of fundamentally reducing any scientific term to terms of physics.

These epistemological assumptions had a remarkable effect when they were transferred to the foundation of human and social sciences, and they continue to do so. In the first place, the social world is considered to be of the same order as the natural world, and so it can be investigated following the same methodology. What is more, the social world is objective, for which reason it is the task of the human and social sciences to know its unvarying laws. The researcher must direct himself towards a knowledge of the effective processes of society as if they were alien and thus independent of his own interpretation.

Fact and not action is the object of study in the positivist field of the human and social sciences. It is here that the weakest point in the whole positivist framework comes out: to speak of social facts, in analogy with natural ones, signifies evading the complex issue over the reasons of action and thus over values, ends, intentions, etc. If however, by fact we mean action (and the difference is only in the term itself), then all that we can claim having denied any sense to reason is that actions are correlated to each other mechanistically: the stimulus of an action would provoke a response on the part of another action. This way of defining action is not simply a partial description of it, but rather the presupposition precluding the possibility of making sense of the action itself.

According to positivism, the social world is described on the basis of a neutral observant language, operating according to rigorous logical procedures and capable of expressing a knowledge of the laws of society. Use of this language would guarantee an element of objectivity for the human and social sciences and provide a representation of the neutral social world with respect to its intentions, values and ends.

The positivist plan of founding the human and social sciences was undoubtedly an ambitious one and it was not just by chance that its influence was remarkable. All the same, it did not succeed in providing laws of society that had certainty, cognitive capacity, or an ability to explain and foresee as the natural sciences had. It is in this very failure of the plan that reactions against positivism emerge; we can characterise these reactions globally with the term "hermeneutic".

In a hermeneutic perspective, the fundamental task of knowledge in the human and social sciences is to enforce the conditions of making the social world totally comprehensible. This understanding is possible if sense is imposed not only upon actions (individual and social) realised in society, but also on the general complex conception of the world, within which reasons are given to justify and explain how these actions happened. We must emphasise the determining importance of the subject's action since he is a bearer of component parts referring to his interpretation of his reality. Consequently man's actions are endowed with sense and this sense can be communicated intersubjectively through continually evolving language, which also expresses subjective components. Thus action cannot be explained without some reference to subjective categories such as intentions, ends, rules, values and so on. Action then, can be explained through the components of the agent's conscience, which are related to his vision of the world. The sense of his actions depends on them, and they in turn play their part in creating the social world. Language is not the 'neutral' representation of this world. Since its role is to express the sense of action, it constitutes the actions themselves in that world. Consequently, language is a constituitive part of the social world which cannot be conceived of or known independently of the concepts inherent in language and the subjective sense they are endowed with. With this type of social world, subjects may have different interpretations, due to the very fact that the elements in their conscience are different. In a hermeneutic perspective, sense is much more widely limited in respect to the limitations recognised by positivists in the human sciences; it is not derived only from experience, but also from a general interpretation of reality. As far as the investigation that I am carrying out on the philosophical bases of masonic thought is concerned, a hermeneutic perspective comprises a general background that cannot be excluded.

By defining the terms 'knowledge' and 'science', positivism has constantly fought against all kinds of metaphysical claims; that is, it has fought against that particular kind of reflection which is unable to justify its own results on the grounds of empirical data, or which forms judgements that experience cannot contradict. Therefore, according to positivism, since all ideas defended by traditional metaphysics are not upheld by an empirical base, they are reveries identifiable in propositions that make no sense whatsoever. Positivism then, criticises both the religious conceptions of the world and the metaphysics of materialism and is constantly searching for a perspective free from all metaphysical presupposition.

A criticism of metaphysics also means a criticism of that part of philosophy which produces metaphysics. These attitudes against metaphysics and traditional philosophy deny cognitive validity to value judgements and normative expressions. Positivists claim there are no objects, events or ways of behaviour in experience that may be labelled 'good' or 'bad', 'just' or 'unjust', just as there is no experience that can force us to accept, with the help of logical procedures, affirmations concerning what one 'must' or 'must not' do. So, for example, the judgement according to which 'human life is an absolute irreplaceable value' cannot be justified in any way on the grounds of experience; it can be accepted or rejected, but in both cases the arbitrariness of the choice must be recognised. We can therefore form value judgements about the world and about man, but we cannot maintain that they are justifiable scientifically, or that they can be founded on something that is not our will. In general, we cannot gain access to the sphere of values through experience. In this way, value judgements are insignificant, since they are neither descriptive propositions nor logical tautologies. Science stands neutral before the sphere of values and this neutrality is understood as a principle and is not limited to a certain stage of scientific development. Even for values (and for *ought-to-be* in general) the same metaphysical considerations made by the positivists are valid. However, if one denies any foundation of sense to *ought-to-be*, values are recognised as having an instrumental role within certain empirical social sciences such as psychology or sociology. So we reach the conviction that ethics (and all other normative disciplines) is a branch of the social sciences, where its role is to direct man's behaviour, while at the same time being denied any autonomy. It follows that a scientific sociology of customs is possible, and also a history of ethical doctrines or moral psychology, but not an autonomous scientific ethic.

On a political and social level, positivism is presented as a pedagogical praxis in the struggle against irrationalisms that disturb social life. It therefore claims that it spreads a scientific attitude among men in respect to its own conceptions of the world, thus contributing to the elimination of irrational prejudices and ideological fanaticisms. Differences in national ideologies at the end of the First World War went a long way towards having scientific verification accepted among intellectuals as well as propagating it as a criterion with which to establish the validity of ideological declarations. In this way, people believed that they were forming a defence for themselves against ideological violence and spreading the spirit of tolerance in democratic social life. Positivists were certain that the attitude of the intellectual, whose convictions were always based on strict scientific thought, would become a model towards which all men should aspire in their education. They recognised, therefore, notable pedagogic qualities in their plan, and considered it capable of impressing toleration, moderation and responsibility on man's mind. From a political point of view, in opposing fascist and racist doctrine, most positivists felt close to social-democratic ideas. They were a reflection of that humanitarian opposition to devastation caused by bloody wars and it was their hope that with the spread of scientific rationality, the disastrous consequences of the ideologies would be mitigated. The generalisation and radicalisation of this hope brought about the birth of a utopia according to which, humanity was to make use of scientific thought to crush once and for all the irrationality of ideology and ensure well-being and happiness to man.

Now that we have given a general outline of the fundamental notions of positivism, let us go on to examine the effect that these ideas had either directly or indirectly on Freemasonry.

We noted earlier that positivism moves from the presupposition that the sciences of man can only be empirical sciences. Consequently, man as an object of scientific investigation is necessarily absorbed into the objects of other empirical sciences. The difference between the object man and the physical object in general is essentially a difference in degree: with respect to the other objects of the external world, man is a more 'complex'object. This difference does not, therefore, justify a methodology of the human and social sciences being any different from that used in the natural sciences. Categories such as 'intentionality', 'ends', 'values', and such like do not, according to positivists, come into the study of this 'complexity'. Consequently, man is denied a projectual capacity; meaning the possibility of conceiving projects (by himself or with others) on the basis of an end and a scale of shared values. Denial of projectuality leads to the denial of the project of initiatic perfection which reflects a principle of masonic thought that cannot be ignored. The positivist conception therefore, precludes the possibility of understanding and explaining man's action (even masonic action) on the grounds of intentional and finalistic reasons, while it brings the sense of action itself back to physical causes which are also external to man.

This conception brings us to another fundamental limitation, which makes it even more unacceptable to masonic thinking: by affirming that the only valid 'image' of man is that which is acquired and formulated exclusively through the contributions of the empirical sciences that study man, the possibility of considering this image as 'ideal', that is a point of reference for man himself in the realisation of his projectuality, is denied. Man acts not only to achieve determined ends but also, and above all on the basis of 'an image of himself', which is regarded as an ideal, and to which he continually compares himself in the planning of his activities. In this way positivism can provide an image of man as he is but not as he *ought-to-be*: it is not at all possible to distinguish in this image between the level of being from the level of how one *ought-to-be*. An important consequence of this limitation is that, in positivism, *there can be no philosophical anthropology*. As I pointed out in Chapter 2, philosophical anthropology concerns a global image of man, based on his nature which is projected towards an end. Since in positivism the image of man is exclusively that which results from the overall contribution of the single empirical sciences that study him, we find that both the totalizing dimension (the horizon of totality) and the dimension of the *ought-to-be* missing, and thus too the possibility of founding a philosophical anthropology. As far as masonic and Christian anthropologies are concerned, we can say that 'positivist philosophical anthropology' is an empty set, bereft of any constituent elements.

These theoretical conclusions can be expressed even through the difficulties that crossed the path of positivism when it was measured against the ethical dimension of man. Indeed, we noted earlier that positivism upheld, at least through the contributions of its authoritative exponents, the possibility of reducing ethics (and normative disciplines) to certain empirical social sciences (psychology and sociology). Well, if on the one hand, this reduction has emphasised the social conditioning of ethics, on the other, it has destroyed any form of autonomy it might have had. Even this theoretical result is unacceptable to the masonic way of thinking, which for its own part, searches in ethics (autonomous) for the source of legitimisation of its actions and projects as we saw in Chapters 2 and 4.

We have another difficulty in our path. Even if they deny the autonomy of ethics on a theoretical level, positivists speak of the betterment of man, and thus admit to some form of pre-understanding of an ethical nature. This betterment of man would be principally associated with scientific progress and the 'good' technical applications it makes. To say that the betterment of man is due to forms of scientific knowledge (and their applications), means that we must begin from the presupposition that scientific knowledge, as such, is something good. But we have seen that value judgements cannot come from experience, which is why one would be forced, in order to make an evaluation, to move away from experience by violating a basic principle of positivism. Furthermore, these difficulties become more evident if technological applications are taken into consideration. On what grounds, indeed, can we affirm that a technical application is good or not? For an answer, it would be necessary to start from a notion of good that is independent of what has been declared by science. At most, science can say it is good in the face of applications that conform to scientific methodology, but it cannot say it is good when independent of an end that is good in itself. Even in this case, the notion of betterment refers us to a value judgement that positivism cannot accept on the basis of its theoretical assumption. These difficulties highlight the inadequacy (with regards to masonic thinking) of some positivist principles such as unity of the sciences and the reduction of having to be to being.

Consequently, positivist conception is fundamentally immanent. The only thing that is true is what we can investigate by means of scientific method, but since this has an empirical basis, what is true is only that which belongs to the level of experience. All that transcends experience has no truth value (it is senseless). Therefore, there is no transcendent dimension. As far as our discussion on

Freemasonry is concerned, it is interesting to note that the negation of transcendence is not exclusively a negation of its ontological valence, but of its axiological valence, needed as a minimal requirement by masonic conception, which admits, on the grounds of its theory of non-exclusive regulativism, that a mason *can* accept the existence of a god given ontologically, since T.G.A.O.T.U. must be understood at least as a transcendent principle. This means that Freemasonry regards acceptance of the ethical order, directed towards T.G.A.O.T.U. as an end and thus as transcendence. The ethical principles are guaranteed by the very assumption of T.G.A.O.T.U., at least in his capacity as a regulative principle. Whereas for positivism, there is no valid ethical experience (with sense) that can be reduced to the level of sensitive experience (naturalistic), Freemasonry recognises an ethic which is justified and guaranteed by the acceptance of T.G.A.O.T.U. as a regulative principle, since it cannot be reduced to an empirical order. Consequently, ethical principles come to be the expression not so much of what man *in actual fact* chooses (as positivism maintains) as the expression of what he chooses on the basis of his own free will directed validly towards good. Transcendence, understood at least in the axiological sense, is a typical constituent element of masonic thinking, but not of positivist conceptions. From this point of view, there is a enormous incompatibility between Freemasonry and positivism (they go in opposite directions). Therefore, Freemasonry is halfway between positivism (understood as an expression of radical immanentism), on the one hand and religion (understood as an exclusive expression of a strong transcendence in the ontological sense), on the other. Consequently, Freemasonry is neither positivism nor religion.

To conclude, while opposing masonic conceptions, positivism has exerted a great influence, and still continues to do so, within certain masonic circles. This is due, above all to the fact that, by moving from scientific universalism its pedagogical and social plan reflects the principles of freedom and tolerance, while it condemns all forms of racism and authoritarianism. Within a socio-political commitment, Freemasonry and positivism are therefore guardians of principles that they both share. This also explains why influential positivists have seen in Freemasonry the ideal environment for propagating and realising their pedagogical syllabus. Yet there are still some remarkable differences on a theoretical level. Here, Freemasonry and positivism find themselves defending irreconcilable positions.

What we have considered so far allows us to characterise a particularly important aspect of science, that of responsibility. But for a more correct understanding of it we must explain its origin and more recent developments.

In the world in which we live, we are very often witness to events, such as the nuclear contamination of Chernobyl or the genetic manipulations of man, which cause us to reflect on science and its applications. The fundamental problem that emerges from these reflections is the following: is science a good thing in itself (as positivists maintain) in the sense that it is completely extraneous to any consequences resulting from its application, or does it make sense only in as far as it contributes to the economical, social, political, ethical and spiritual development of man as well?

From its modern origins, science has claimed a fundamental human right: that of researching freely. In this sense, it represents the concrete fulfillment of man to pursue his search for truth without being constrained by the limitations imposed by State authorities or religious dogma. Therefore, modern science has been able to develop thanks to an attitude of free thought which has left a deep mark on western culture in the last two centuries.

The request for freedom for science and its applications finds valid justification in the principle of tolerance on the basis of which the scientist assumes an attitude of liberality in respect to all those, whatever their language, culture and religion, who belong to the scientific community. Tolerance becomes, in turn, the presupposition of universality. The scientist, a firm believer in freedom, tolerance and universality raises these principles to fundamental categories of interpretation not only of science but also of the whole of reality.

Consequently, science is seen as an expression of public knowledge, open to discussion and reflection on the basis of professional competence and methodological rigour. Furthermore, the scientist must possess the highest level of intellectual honesty and be ready to recognise his own mistakes and accept criticism from his opponents, as long as it is scientifically founded.

This way of interpreting science and the scientist reflects an ideality, an *ought-to-be*, one should make for. Therefore scientists have not always acted in accordance with the intellectual and moral model. In fact, the history of science is full of examples of dogmatism, intolerance, and personal ambition, yet this does not alter the validity of the model, just as a moral or religious doctrine preserves its whole meaning even if some of its disciples behave in such a way as to violate its basic precepts.

This explains, in particular, that kind of veneration for science which was prevalent in western culture from the nineteenth to the first half of the present century. Such veneration, which has even led to radical forms of scientism, was, as we have already seen, one of the principal attitudes of positivism in the fight against the irrationalisms which trouble social life.

In brief, science has appeared in modern times as one of man's most noble enterprises, and as such completely free to search for its truth. It therefore appears to have a kind of *non-responsibility* in respect to what others might do with its conquests, discoveries and results.

This is where science emerges as a myth of neutrality. Science is good in itself. Therefore, its aim is to search for truth independently of anything else. No-one, not even the State or the Church, can limit its development.

This image of science, which, from a philosophical point of view finds complete expression in positivism, underwent a radical change towards the middle of the present century. This was particularly due to the explosion of the first atom bomb, which pricked the moral conscience of the scientist who had to come to terms with his involvement in the application of scientific discoveries. There are many well-known cases of scientists feeling truly morally guilty as a result of this event. And yet the construction of the atom bomb as a destructive weapon was nothing new. Indeed, scientific discoveries have always found application in the history of humanity even in the military sphere and in the production of ever more powerful weapons. However we are led to evaluate this event in a completely different way with respect to the past by the idea of self-destruction of mankind thanks to certain applications that are carried out on scientific discoveries: it is the scientist's conscience that, for the first time, tells him he may well be *jointly responsible* for the destruction of his fellow man. In his search for pure and simple scientific truth he was responsible only for the way in which the discoveries were reached but not for the use others might have made of them. Now, the scientist must do more than just control what happens within science. He feels his moral conscience pricking making him see even what happens outside science at the hands of others. Scientific truth is no longer enough for him and he searches for a wider truth, which includes scientific truth, and directs it towards the achievement of one of man's aims.

This process of revision concerns not only pure science but applied science as well. The idea that applied science is nothing other than the exploitation of scientific knowledge for the benefit of mankind falls on stony ground, due not only to incorrect application, but also to the dangerous consequences and uncontrollable future damage the same useful appplications may incur (as at Chernobyl). Contamination of the environment and the risk of compromising the future of mankind following a wrong experiment are just two of the important topics that come under frequent discussion, and as a result science is no longer considered something good in itself and, like all other human activities, reveals its own ambivalences and dangers.

In this way, two different and opposing scientific perspectives emerge. Some scholars maintain that scientific activity reflects a rigorous and neutral search for truth, which cannot be affected by anything external to science, such as factors of a political, social or religious nature. On the other hand, others assert that science has always been the expression of power (political, economic, ethical, religious), and that it is deceptive to believe that it may exclusively produce a credible and unbiased knowledge. I propose that both these conceptions are largely one-sided and therefore capture only in part what science really is. Thus it is wrong to make each originate from a general point of view, since the validity of the one would exclude the validity of the other. Consequently, a unitary vision emerges on the basis of which science proves to be characterised by both the above-mentioned points of view.

The problem of responsibility is present in this unitary perspective. The responsibility of science means therefore that the scientist is fully aware that his search for truth is also a form of participation in the appropriate global reality. In this sense, it is mainly manifested as the uprooting of old evaluative criteria and birth of new values.

Reference to values directly affects ethical reflection, in which case one may have an ethic capable of directing the choices of scientific research and regulating its operative capacities. It follows that science cannot develop completely without facing reference values that are compatible with other values that exist in a given social system and in which it lives with. The values of science will have to *integrate* with other values given in a particular society. An ethical theory of science must therefore have a *totality* of values as its starting point and, within it, isolate and correlate typically scientific ones.

In brief, science is not good in itself (as positivists maintain) but only becomes so in relation to man, to his survival and global betterment, to his economic, political, social, cultural, aesthetic, ethical and spiritual betterment.

At this point we ask ourselves: what standpoint does Freemasonry take with respect to science? The question we ought to pose is whether, according to Masonic thought, science is good in itself or whether it is good only in as far as it contributes to the betterment of man. Our investigation in the previous chapters allows us to assert that Freemasonry, albeit an initiatic society, feels deeply bound to facing the problems of contemporaneity not only so as to understand them but also in order to solve them. And in doing so, it takes inspiration from its anthropological philosophy, that is from its image of man. Indeed, masonic anthropology is compared with the above-mentioned conceptions of science. From a first and superficial analysis, it seems that

Freemasonry shares the notion of science understood as something good in itself. In fact, both the scientist and the mason have in common freedom, tolerance, brotherhood, universality, and the search for truth (never revealed and absolute). But the analogies go no further. Since freedom, tolerance and brotherhood are notions rooted in immanence, there is a fundamental difference between the positivist scientist and the mason in the very way immanence is understood. Whilst for the former, all that has sense boils down, either directly or indirectly, to immanence, for the latter the sense to be conferred on reality is wider and is a consequence of a regulative principle on the basis of which transcendence regulates immanence, whereas immanence tends towards transcendence in a continual and infinite process. The assumption of regulative transcendence on the part of masonic thought indicates a line of demarcation between Freemasonry and science understood in a positivist sense (a science good in itself). Consequently, Freemasonry shares and defends the notion of science as something good only if it is directed towards the global betterment of man, in other words, towards his physical, biological, economic, social, political, aesthetic, ethical end spiritual betterment. For the mason, the values of science are relative values to be placed alongside all other values in a given society, starting from a unitary point of view provided by masonic anthropology. The supreme aim of this anthropology is the ethical and spiritual realisation of man.

Chapter 8

Freemasonry and the Roman Catholic Church

The image of Freemasonry I have outlined in the previous chapters has English and American Freemasonry (Constitutions, Landmarks, Acts, Declarations) to thank for its foundation, but it transcended this to become a valid way of thinking for all masonic circles. It therefore represents an *ideality* with which to make comparisons between individual masonic societies as they have actually existed, as part of the totality of Freemasonry, but differentiated from each other with respect to tradition, language and culture.

I intend to use this image to interpret the relationship that has developed between Freemasonry on the one hand, and the Roman Catholic Church and State (in their widest sense), on the other. The aim of this and the following chapter is to examine these relationships.

As far as the relationship with the Roman Catholic Church is concerned, let me remind you of the conclusions we came to in Chapter 6, that a) Freemasonry is not a religion, and b) there is no incompatibility between belonging to Freemasonry and professing a religious faith.

Points a) and b) are very closly linked since the truth of b) presupposes the truth of a). Thus there may be conciliation between Freemasonry and religion only if Freemasonry is *not* a religion. This should already be clear from the previous chapters (particularly Chapter 6). However, the Catholic Church has recently reproposed the thesis that the two are not reconcilable. So now we must carefully examine this thesis and the reasons for it.

First of all, let us see how the thesis of incompatibility has been outlined within the Roman Catholic Church in more recent times. The most authoritative recent act is the *Declaratio* on Freemasonry by Cardinal J. Ratzinger, Prefect of the Congregation for the Doctrine of the Faith, issued on 6th November 1983. Since all subsequent reflections refer to this document, it is worth presenting it here in full, translated from the Latin.

Declaration on Freemasonry: The question has been asked whether the judgement of the Church has changed at all with regards to Freemasonry since it is not expressly mentioned in the new Code of Canon Law as it was in the earlier Code.

This Congregation is able to respond that this circumstance is due to an editorial criterion followed for other associations equally not mentioned, since they are included in wider categories.

Therefore the negative judgement of the Church is unchanged with regards to masonic societies, because their principles have always been considered incompatible with the doctrine of the Church and thus adherence to it is still prohibited. The faithfuls who belong to masonic societies are in a grave state of sin and may not take Holy Communion.

It is not up to the local Church authorities to pass any judgement on the nature of masonic societies which might imply any form of revocation of what has been established above; this is in accord with the Declaration of this Holy Congregation of 17th February 1981 (cf. AAS 73/ 1981/ pp. 240-241).

In the course of the audience accorded to the undersigned Cardinal Prefect, the High Pontiff John Paul II approved the present Declaration, which was previously formulated in the ordinary meeting of this Holy Congregation, and ordered that it should be published. Rome, dated November 26th 1983 in the seat of the Holy Congregation for the Doctrine of the Faith. Signed by Cardinal Joseph Ratzinger.

On February 23rd 1985, the *Osservatore Romano* published an anonymous front page three column article (expressing however, the official position of the Congregation for the Doctrine of the Faith), entitled: 'Reflections one year after the Declaration of the Congregation for the Doctrine of the Faith. Incompatibility between the Christian Faith and Masonry'.

The reflections of this document are essentially of three kinds: theoretical, practical and socio-cultural.

The considerations of the theoretical kind can be analysed on two different levels. The first finds expression in the following quotation: 'Above all, it must be remembered that the community of 'free masons' and their moral obligations are presented as a progressive system of symbols of a very binding nature. The strict discipline of the occult pervading it further strengthens the weight of interaction of its signs and ideas. This atmosphere of secrecy involves for the enrolled, above all, the risk of becoming an instrument of strategies unknown to them'. This passage concerns the discipline of the mystery that is in force in Freemasonry, or so the authors of the document claim, and provokes a lack of respect for the human being due to the initiation secret. Again from a theoretical point of view, the second level of reflections finds explanation in the following passage: 'Even if one asserts that relativism is not accepted as dogma, nonetheless a relativistic symbolic conception is in fact proposed, and therefore, far from being able to be eliminated, the relativizing value of this moral ritual community proves, on the contrary, to be determining'. In this context, the different religious communities to which the individual members of the Lodges belong can only be considered simple institutionalisations of a wider elusive truth. Thus the value of these institutionalisations appears to be inevitably relative to this wider truth, which is manifested in the community of good will, or in other words, in the masonic brotherhood. This quotation affirms that Freemasonry assumes a *relativistic* attitude, since it places all religious faiths (and therefore the Roman Catholic faith too) on the same level. Here a vision is expressed according to which Freemasonry represents a form of thought directed towards a truth (not completely known since it is enclosed within the secret) that is 'wider', global, not possessed nor can be so by any church in particular. It is said that for the mason, churhes are religious institutions where a particular modality is realised. A modality which carries one through symbolic forms of sensitive representation to a truth that is always wider in respect to these forms of representation. On the other hand, this wider truth characterises masonic thought. If the problem of truth is considered in this form, then there can be no compatibility between Freemasonry and the Roman Catholic Church, since the Roman Catholic Church is reduced to a particular form (and this a partial if not an erroneous one) of representation of a wider truth that only Freemasonry has the right to claim.

Reflections of the second kind are mainly of a practical nature and the consequence of the relativistic attitude mentioned above. In fact we can read the following in the document: "However, it is not possible for the Catholic Christian to live his relationship with God in a dual modality, that is, dividing it into a humanitarian super-confessional form and an internal Christian form. He cannot cultivate two kinds of relationship with God, nor can he express his relationship with the Creator through two kinds of symbolic forms. That would be something completely different from the collaboration (obvious to him) with all those engaged in doing good, even if from different principles. Yet a Catholic Christian cannot at the same time take part in the full communion of the Christian fraternity and regard his Christian brother from a masonic perspective as a 'profane' ". This then, refers to the case where a Catholic Christian is also a member of a Masonic Lodge and the idea is expressed according to which, if a man accepts to become a mason and remain a Catholic Christian, then he holds with God a relationship with a dual meaning: as a mason and as a Christian. The result is a practical incompatibility.

Again with regards to practical considerations, the document contains an explicit reference to relativism in its assertion that 'Even if, as we have already said, there were no explicit obligation to profess relativism as a doctrine, nevertheless, by its very intrinsic logic, the relativizing strength of such a brotherhood has the capacity to transform the structure of the act of faith so radically that it cannot be accepted by the Christian, "whose faith is dear to him" (Leo XIII)'

Reflections of the third kind, referring to contemporary mentality, are of a socio-cultural nature. The document has this to say: 'he upsetting of the act of faith in its fundamental structure, is for the most part done gently and unnoticeably: the firm adherence to the truth of God, revealed in the Church, becomes a mere belonging to an institution, considered a particular expressive form beside other more expressive ones, just as possible and valid more or less, of man's directing his steps towards eternal life. The temptation to take this direction is so much stronger today since it corresponds in advance to certain conditions that are prevalent in contemporary mentality. It is commonly believed today that truth cannot be known, but at the same time it is considered as essential part of the general crisis of the times'

Let us now try to examine the reflections expounded according to the principles of masonic thought.

As we have seen, the reflections of a theoretical nature concern the notion of 'wider truth' where Freemasonry is considered a *super-religion* and the notion of a 'discipline of the occult' in which masons run the risk of becoming an instrument of strategies unknown to them. We will begin with the first notion.

The declaration in which Freemasonry is seen as a super-religion withholding a global truth is totally alien to masonic thought, as I have had occasion to show in the course of this investigation, and as the Board of the United Grand Lodge of England stressed when it declared that 'Freemasonry is not a religion, nor a syncretism of religions'. This alone would be enough to prove false what is stated in the Catholic document. Nevertheless, I intend to make further considerations on this document, given its importance in subsequent reflections as well.

The mistake of attributing to Freemasonry the typical characteristics of a super-religion seems to derive from a certain interpretation of deism, that is of that particular form of universal religion based on the reason all men agree on, from which Anderson took inspiration when he wrote the masonic Constitutions. There are two points to note here:

1 deism is not a super religion but represents the point at which all particular religions meet and

2 deism has indeed characterised the development of Freemasonry but only in the period between 1717 and 1813.

Therefore, even in the hypothesis that deism coincides with the presumed super-religion that the authors of the Catholic document speak of, this could not have any relative historical value. In any case, it is completely alien to contemporary masonic thought. When nowadays we speak of Freemasonry and its religious foundations, our aim is to maintain that a mason *can have* a religion (according to the theory of non-exclusive regulativism) but not that Freemasonry is a religion. Therefore reference in the Catholic document to a masonic truth wider than that included in each single religion, can only be considered wrong.

If Freemasonry is not a religion then the accusation of relativism falls too. Our investigation so far allows us to state that Freemasonry does not possess a wider truth, of which the truth of the single religions are partial manifestations. Consequently, these partial truths are not to be associated with a global truth, which Freemasonry should possess. However we have yet to examine the judgement of relativism that, according to the Catholic document, Freemasonry is supposed to give to individual religions, irrespective of whether it held a truth wider than the one they defended or not. Let us try to answer the following questions: does Freemasonry place all religions on the same level, or does it differentiate between them according to some evaluative criterion? First of all, Freemasonry does not express evaluations of particular religions, neither does it propose to rate them on an hierarchical scale. In accordance with its point of view regarding man on an exclusively ethical level, Freemasonry regards all particular religions as having equal dignity. This means that Freemasonry is not prepared to make any declaration (it does not even have the competence to do so) on the content of truth of individual religions; rather it aims to declare itself on the ethical principles each religion defends in order to identify possible points of agreement with its own, according to which the project of betterment of the mason is realised. The comparison on an exclusively ethical level is justified by the fact that masonic thought is not presented as a global conception of man. Indeed it is because Freemasonry does not aspire to so much that it does not have its own truth to compare to that of individual religions. Only its proposal for the betterment of man, which for Freemasonry has an exclusively ethical meaning, may be compared to the ethical principles which individual religions uphold.

The discussion must go further than this, even beyond the limits of the following brief reflections, because this is where the thesis of incompatibility holds good or fails. If, as we have seen, there can be no incompatibility between Catholic and Masonic thought on the theoretical level of the global conception of the world, it is equally true that Freemasonry upholds a determined ethically inspired anthropology. Masonic ritual itself is a symbolic form of this, for the very reason that Freemasonry does not propose a global interpretation of reality. Judging compatibility or incompatibility between the Catholic faith and masonic thought therefore means, in short, judging whether basic principles of Catholic ethics and those of masonic ethics are compatible or not. But is it possible to circumscribe a group of ethical principles of Freemasonry sufficient to characterise the idea of ethical commitment, allowing at the same time the setting up of a discussion on concrete grounds, at least in a preliminary approximation, of whether they are compatible or not?

When in Chapter 6 I defined the relationship between ethical masonry and the ethics of individual religions, I maintained that one can justifiably assert that there are ethical principles concerning the actions of the mason as such, since masonic actions are those actions that aim at his betterment as a mason and are therefore worthy of consideration in respect to the masonic regulative ideal. But what are these ethical principles of the mason? Can they be listed? And can such a list of ethical principles be compared with that of the Catholic Church?

It seems that the quintuple–*Freedom, Tolerance, Brotherhood, Transcendence, Initiatic Secret*–comprising the fundamental elements of masonic anthropology, consists of the source from which to enucleate the basic ethical principles of Freemasonry, principles which each mason should feel he cannot give up beyond the cultural and historical differences that their application may incur. As we have maintained in the previous chapters, the anthropology originating from the quintuple is essentially ethical, characterised in a first approximation by two general principles: the principle according to which man should be accorded recognition of his dignity of being free to express his own ideas and realise them respecting the freedom of others, and the principle of tolerance, which is a consequence of the former by virtue of the respect due to every man.

Now, since these two principles concern a relation of reciprocal respect between individuals, they may be called moral (in the strict sense of the word) in contrast to those having a more purposeful prescriptive content, for which reason they can be called ethical (in the strict sense of the word). Therefore they are without doubt compatible with Catholic ethical principles. Even the Catholic Church fully recognises itself in these two moral principles, which they see as cornerstones in the ethical conception of the person. On the other hand, each ethical conception also includes ethical principles (in the strict sense of the word), that is principles which do not say what one must not do (like moral principles) but what it is good to do. Masonic ethics specifically include principles of this kind. And so we should turn our attention to these given that, even if there may be no agreement on moral issues, this may not necessarily be the case with ethical principles (in the strict sense).

One might then suppose that masonic ethical principles can all be contained in the two subsequent components of the quintuple, brotherhood and transcendence. This pervasive ethical value of masonic thought is in fact constituted by a search for values which, among those advanced by individuals or groups, guarantees the betterment (on all levels) of the whole of mankind into a spirit of peaceful accord and reciprocal tolerance.

Therefore the placing of brotherhood at the head of masonic anthropology means starting from the conviction that a community must be realised which ideally directs itself to the good of all and is ideally capable of welcoming into it all men as brothers.

Naturally a formulation of the principle of brotherhood, independent of the specification of what is good for man, is not enough to evaluate its positivity with respect to the good maintained by the Catholic Church. Yet this is where Catholic authorities have least confidence in the practical philosophy of Freemasonry. Nevertheless good should be understood in general by the mason as good for man, where man is defined also by his ideal relation of tension towards transcendence. This is where the fourth element of the anthropological quintuple makes its mark. The image of man it describes cannot be kept separate from the transcendent dimension, which is why it is totally incorrect to attribute to Freemasonry a conception of man reduced to the conditions of a biological and economic life. Masonic axiology recognises in man, not only vital and useful values but also the highest spiritual values since it conceives the spirit as being projected towards the *ought-to-be* that is itself spiritual. One might discuss whether there are also some specific religious values among these. It is true that Freemasonry does not include them, since it does not consider them to be a constitutive part of its anthropology, yet it does not exclude them either, since it judges them to be part of a dimension that is alien to its own sphere of interest and competence. But if the Catholic Church does not exclude 'that collaboration with all those that have committed themselves to carrying out good, even if from different principles', it is not clear why the Church itself declares incompatibility between Catholic and masonic ethics, when the latter concerns the realisation, at least in part (and according to particular modalities) of the same good pursued by the Catholic Church.

A further point of discussion comes from the presence in the anthropological quintuple of the initiatic secret. Are there perhaps hidden in this secret some incompatible ethical principles or at least principles that they may not be analysed for the very fact that they are secret? Leaving aside for the moment the practical significance of this objection, it should be stressed here that the initiatic secret concerns the concrete ritual *modalities* of initiation for the betterment of the mason from an ethical point of view, whereas the principles at its base can be related to the first four elements of the quintuple. There is no added ethical content but only ritual prescriptions that are suitable for promoting the masonic ethical ideal which has *already been defined* in the principles exposed.

If we analyse the above-mentioned theoretical considerations, we are led to conclude that there is no relativism in masonic thinking, since a) Freemasonry does not claim any global vision of man and a wider truth, b) its anthropology is essentially an ethical anthropology whose theoretical principles are all compatible with Catholic ethical principles. The theory of compatibility follows from points a) and b).

Let us now move on to the second level of theoretical considerations regarding the secret. The document has this to say: 'The moral obligations (of masons) are presented as a progressive system of symbols of a very binding nature. The strict discipline of the occult dominating it, further strengthens the weight of interaction of signs and ideas. This air of secrecy involves above all for the enrolled, the risk of becoming an instrument of strategies unknown to them.

This passage expresses two doubts: a) the secret is harmful to the human, b) the secret allows no comparison between the scale of ethical principles of Freemasonry and those of the Roman Catholic Church. As far as a) is concerned, we must return to what was said in Chapter 6, where it was declared that the mason was bound to accept the authority of the co-optant before being admitted to the initiatic secret, which therefore cannot be examined by those who aspire to enter Freemasonry. The question we posed in Chapter 6 comes to light again: is this way of proceeding harmful to the autonomy of the person who represents the basic principle of the Christian ethical theory? We have already established that the answer must be no, since keeping secret the contents of the initiation is not the fruit of an unjustified will of the co-optant tending to bind the will of the other, but the necessary condition through which the contents of the initiatic secret may be revealed. In this way the autonomy of the person is not jeopardised in the secret. As for b) a doubt is expressed that, if the project of the ethical betterment of the mason is held within the secret, then one may not even speak of compatibility since the very possibility of comparing the ethical principles of Freemasonry with those of the Catholic Church is lacking. How can the Church pronounce itself on compatibility with an unknown scale of values? Here we must stress again the nature of the initiatic secret. It does not concern ethical principles, which are defined elsewhere, but the modalities with which these values are realised through a progressive procedure of initiation to interiorise them. We must again emphasise the fact that the secret *does not* alter the meaning of the moral and ethical principles which are at its base but simply reflects a modality of realisation. The mason improves his own ethical condition by continuing along the road of initiation which is characterised by the secret. Consequently the secret is not for masons 'an instrument of strategies unknown to them' neither is it 'harmful to the autonomy of the person'.

These are my comments on the theoretical reflections contained in the Catholic document. The reflections of the second (practical) and third (socio-cultural) types are consequent to those of the first (theoretical). There is *coherence* in the Catholic document between the three types of reflection in the sense that the truth of the second and third kind of reflection is a consequence of the truth of those of the first type. But the comments to the reflections of the first (theoretical) type have shown that the central points of these reflections can at least be discussed, in that a) Freemasonry is not a religion (it does not have a wider truth and does not aspire to a global vision of man), and b) does not profess a form of relativism, and c) its ethical principles, in the limits of its competence, do not oppose Catholic ones. It follows that the whole document of the *Osservatore Romano* does not appear to have a firm base in its assumptions and therefore, objections can be made to its conclusions.

Before coming to the end of our reflections on the document in the *Osservatore Romano*—which can be compared to the United Grand Lodge of England for its contents and authority—it is worth explaining its historical and doctrinal background.

Both the *Declaratio* of 1983 and the *Reflections* of 1985 found inspiration in a document against the Freemasonry published by German bishops on 8th April 1980. This document in fact refers to the Encyclical *Humanum Genus* of Leo XIII (20th April 1884) where it is affirmed that 'the teaching of the Church denounced the philosophical ideas and moral conceptions of Freemasonry opposing Catholic doctrine' (this passage is also reported in the *Reflections* of 1985), and to the *Letter to the Italian People* (8th December 1892) in which Leo XIII wrote: 'Let us remember that Christianity and Freemasonry are essentially incompatible just as joining one necessarily means separating oneself from the other' (this passage too is written in the *Reflections* of 1985). I would like to stress that the documents of excommunication issued by Leo XIII against Freemasonry are found in the final phase of dissidence between Freemasonry and the Catholic Church and they repeat all the accusations against Freemasonry formulated by the Popes who preceded him. Let us remember only that Pius IX and Leo XIII spoke more than four hundred times in their documents against Freemasonry which in many cases, came to be identified with the Carbonari and other patriotic secret societies fighting at that time for the unity of Italy and against the temporal power of the Popes. Identifying Freemasonry with societies in league against the Church and against legitimate civil authorities can only be understood in reference to the so-called 'Roman question', that is, to the loss of the papal States where the two powers, civil and ecclesiastic, were one and the same person—the Pope.

However, the documents of excommunication of Freemasonry can be dated much earlier.

The first bull of excommunication against Freemasonry, known as 'In Eminenti Apostolatus Specula', was issued by Pope Clement XII on 28th April 1738. Since it was taken up again in subsequent encyclicals as well, it needs to be examined in detail, at least with respect to the motivations of the accusation:

1 *Masons are men of every religion.* The Catholic Church, which is reputed to possess the only true religion, cannot accept the idea of being placed with all other religions on the same level.
2 *Masons manifest an appearance of moral rectitude.* The state of need, in which humanity finds itself after original sin, can be removed not through any form of natural honesty, but through the grace which leads to salvation.
3 *Masons are strictly bound to each other on the basis of a secret pact.* The Church, which wishes to redeem humanity, can only view all that is shrouded in secret with suspicion.
4 *Masons take on obligations by swearing on the Bible and they promise to punish traitors.* The Church cannot allow any man to search for revenge and realise it in a truculent manner.
5 *In many States masonic societies have already been long banned for the reason that they are against the safety of the realm.* In a time when kings and Popes supported each other, this motivation was ideologically very strong and supported.
6 *And for other just and reasonable motives known to us (the Pope) we have established and decreed that the said societies of free masons should be condemned and prohibited.* We could make thousands of suppositions about the motive behind this statement but the most credible one is accusing masonic societies of irreligious practice.

With Clement XII there begins a long list anti-masonic Popes. On 18th May 1751, Benedict XIV (the pope who corresponded with the most eminent illuminists, among whom was the mason Voltaire) renewed and further worsened the condemnation of Freemasonry through the papal bull 'Providas'.

The Popes of the nineteenth century intensified the fight against Freemasonry. In 1814 Pius VII had fixed on church doors a new bull against Freemasonry, which provoked persecution and arrest in some States of Latin America . In 1823 Leo XII issued a bull 'Quo Graviora Mala' which incited Spanish and Portuguese Chancelleries against Freemasonry, after which seven Spanish masons were taken by surprise during an initiation ceremony and hanged. Even Pius VIII, in his only year as Pope, excommunicated masons. So did his successor Gregorius XVI. With Pius IX relations between the Freemasonry and the Church were even further embittered and even more complicated. For an understanding of the role carried out by this Pope in respect to Freemasonry the reader is referred to an excellent study by Don Rosario Esposito *Pius IX—The Church in Conflict with the World.* With the celebration of the second Vatican Council, the Church abandoned its attitude of refusal and aprioristic condemnation that was characteristic in the past of its relations with the modern world and showed itself willing to discuss and collaborate with men of all ideologies and religious beliefs. The most significant conciliatory document in this light is without doubt the pastoral Constitution *Gaudium et Spes* of Paul VI on the Church in the contemporary world. In it he affirmed, among other things: 'The community of Christians feels really and intimately in agreement with mankind and his history. For this reason, the second Vatican Council has penetrated deeper into the mystery of the Church and now does not hesitate to address its message only to the children of the Church and all those who invoke the name of Christ, but to all men'. In Chapter 21 (Attitude of the Church towards Atheism) he also affirmed that: 'While the Church totally refuses atheism, it nevertheless sincerely recognises that all men, whether they be believers or non believers, must help to correctly construct the world in which they have to live together: this, frankly speaking, can only come about through a loyal and prudent dialogue'. These conciliatory declarations echo the encyclical *Ecclesiam Suam* in which Paul VI outlined the image of a church open to dialogue: 'The Church must be ready to uphold a dialogue with all men of good will, within and without its own environment. No-one is alien to its heart. No-one is indifferent for its ministery. No-one is an enemy unless he himself wants to be'. In this atmosphere of availability towards the world, the Church assumes an attitude of practical tolerance even to Freemasonry, to whom it acknowledges acceptance of the transcendent principle in the Grand Architect of the Universe. This period of dialogue between Freemasonry and the Catholic Church was marked by the commitment of some ecclesiastics, authoritative scholars of masonic history, such as Don Rosario Esposito, Father Giovanni Caprile and Don Franco Molinari. The meeting, which took place in Savona on 15th June 1969, was particularly important. In it Giordano Gamberini, Grand Master of Italian Freemasonry of Palazzo Giustiniani, confronted Don Esposito on the relations between Freemasonry and the Catholic Church, in the presence of a thousand masons and Christians. The dialogue between Freemasonry and the Catholic Church has never been interrupted. Recently (8th April 1986) a conference took place at the North East Turin Rotary Club entitled *The Moral Conscience of Man Today* which had as speakers the Grand Master Armando Corona and the Jesuit Federico Weber as well as the participation of the philosopher Vittorio Mathieu and the historian Aldo Mola. The discussion reproposed research into all that, between Freemasonry and the Catholic Church, can favour a collaboration for the realisation of projects whose aim is the ethical betterment of contemporary man.

It must also be remembered that in the new Code of Canon Law, article 2335 was abolished; this was the article prohibiting Catholics from joining masonic societies under penalty of excommunication. One might wonder whether the meaning of this omission is to be identified with the fact that even before this, the Catholic Church had removed excommunication from Freemasonry. As we have already noted, the intention on the other hand, of the *Declaratio* of the Congregation for the Doctrine of the Faith was to stress the negative feeling of the Church as regards Freemasonry making the omission of the article in question depend on purely editorial criteria. However, it seems to us that a re-examination of the basic principles of Freemasonry, such as we have undertaken here, might allow the dialogue between Freemasonry and the Catholic Church to be started up again on new grounds. In this respect, it is very important to note that the Catholic Church today is one of the few bodies in the world claiming the theory of incompatibility. In fact, not only the highest exponents of non-Christian religions (Judaism, Islam, etc), but also Anglican, Orthodox and Lutheran bishops have adhered to Freemasonry, thus resolving favourably the theory of compatibility. Few examples are needed to confirm this: Fisher, Primate of the Anglican Church, and Atenagora, Patriarch of the Orthodox Church, with whom Pope John XXIII began an ecumenical dialogue in a climate of fraternal comprehension, were masons.

To conclude these brief observations, we can only hope that the Catholic Church, following the example of other great universal religions and Christian confessions, will make an effort to overcome its historical diffidence and be able to consider Freemasonry for what it really is today.

Chapter 9

Freemasonry and the State

Modern Freemasonry, which took its inspiration from a specific philosophical anthropology outlined in the previous chapters, greatly influenced the formation of modern society. It was opposed and persecuted for this role, especially by the Catholic Church, who saw in it an expression of 'irreligious practice'. But what the Church condemned was in fact a new means of organising the modern State, that could only be imposed by affirming the principles of freedom, tolerance and justice, which were incompatible with political despotism and religious fanaticism. In fact, the Prince, who considered himself to be invested by the divinity of his own sovereignty, could not treat peoples hostile to his prerogatives on a basis of equality, while the Church, which believed itself to be the holder of absolute truth, could not tolerate living with heretical nations. Consequently it was necessary to destroy these forms of despotism and fanaticism. Only in this way could the new organisation of the State be affirmed on a cosmopolitan and universal foundation, and thus a programme put to work, with a view to realising freedom of thought and culture, equality of citizens before the law, and a closer relationship between the peoples. And finally, the secularisation of the State was requested, that is the negation of any religious authority in the political and civil field.

In this formative operation of modern society, the role carried out by Freemasonry was in some ways decisive. It welcomed into its Lodges men who were full of progressive ideals and united them in a project directed towards the triumph of principles of political freedom and religious tolerance. The secret strengthened this bond, since masons were able to dedicate themselves to its realisation and transmission to new generations without running the risk of being condemned as heretics or subversives. In this way, Freemasonry was an implacable adversary of absolutism and committed itself with all its force to constructing and asserting the parliamentary system. By applying the cosmopolitan principle, it preached universal allegiance against selfish politics which it considered a natural enemy to every race.

It was bitterly attacked and persecuted for this activity. In the previous chapter, I noted the persecutions the Catholic Church carried out by means of numerous documents of excommunication. More than two centuries were to pass before the Church could adopt those political and social ideals advocated by the Freemasonry and before it could include them in its own doctrine regarding the State and society. However in order to understand why the civil states persecuted Freemasonry, we must reconsider the historical conditions that accompanied its creation and its early modern development.

As we have already seen, the second Charge of the Constitutions of Anderson contains the affirmation that 'a mason is a peaceable subject to the Civil Powers, wherever he resides or works, and is never to be concerned in plots and conspiracies against the peace and welfare of the Nation'. Since this declaration has been a source of ambiguity, we must explain it further. First of all, we must say that it was formulated within a particular historical context, characterised by dissidence, in England, between the royal family of Hanover, on the one hand and the supporters of James Francis Edward Stuart, or James III for the Jacobites on the other. With supporters of both factions in the English Lodges, attempts were made to avoid conflict by protecting both.

So can the above declaration, understood as an expression of particular historical contingencies, be generalised? That is, can it be supposed valid for all present and future historical situations? In other words, can it constitute a general principle without exception? If its unconditional validity were admitted, then one would have to request that masons be obliged to respect any civil state power, whether democratic or tyrannical. But then, how can faithfulness or indifference to tyranny be reconciled with masonic philosophical anthropology which postulates freedom itself among the fundamental elements constituting a mason? Freedom and tyranny are not compatible with each other, indeed they are openly contradictory. Therefore, Freemasonry cannot be indifferent to tyranny.

Here, I would like to point out that the mistake of considering the second Charge of Anderson as an absolute and unconditional principle originated from a wrong interpretation of the principle of tolerance intended as indifferentism (see my definition of tolerance). On this basis, for the very reason that they were indifferent to any conception of the State (democratic or authoritarian), masons were obliged always to remain faithful to it. This misunderstanding is even more serious than the previous one. As I have claimed several times, Freemasonry is not indifferent nor agnostic: it has a precise vision of man and society. If this is true, then the second Charge of Anderson must be reformulated as follows: 'A mason is a peaceable subject to those Civil Powers *that guarantee the expression of fundamental freedom*' (the part in italics represents the specification). If this were not true, then it would not be possible to understand why, for example,

American masons (Washington, Jefferson, Franklin and others), after having accepted the Constitutions of Anderson (that were spread throughout the colonies by Franklin himself), conspired and declared war against the Motherland. Furthermore, it would still not be clear why masons from all over the world, in different times, have fought against all forms of tyranny. And finally, it would be difficult to understand the thoughts and actions of those masons who dedicated their own lives to affirming the principles that made it possible to pass from a medieval and authoritarian type of society to a society founded on the rights of man and nations. It is in fact because masons are authors of these principles that they have been persecuted. Condemnations and persecutions have therefore a profound motivation, which is for Freemasonry a source of immense pride. Democratic States should not fear Freemasonry, for it will always be a precious collaborator in solving the most urgent of human and social problems. On the other hand, despotic States should fear Freemasonry, because it will fight them with all its might.

The considerations we have developed so far are confirmed historically. In the previous chapter, we discussed why the Catholic Church condemned Freemasonry. One reason was because the Church tended to defend the temporal power of the papacy. However, it was not the first in its role as preserver of the privileges of the *Ancien Régime*, to order persecutions. Even before Clement XII's encyclical *In eminenti* other States had already condemned Freemasonry. The most ancient document of condemnation against Freemasonry was issued by the Magistrate of Amsterdam on 30th November 1735. The resolution of the General States of Holland bears the same date. A similar resolution was adopted by the Major Council of the City of Geneva at the beginning of March 1736. At the end of the same month, the police in Paris prohibited public bodies from giving hospitality to masonic meetings. On 21st October 1737, there followed a decree of the Prince Elector Palatinate. Chronologically speaking, the encyclical 'In eminenti' is therefore, only the sixth official document condemning Freemasonry.

Freemasonry was persecuted for the choice it made in favour of the principles of tolerance, freedom and equality. This was a conscious and responsible choice, which is why the negative consequences that it was to meet have never been ignored. It is, therefore, misleading to speak of unjust persecutions in its regard. Freemasonry intends to change the world and has not drawn back in the face of the condemnations and persecutions that some States, preserving ancient privileges, have directed toward it. On the other hand, it is important to try to understand why such persecution was justified. Among these, the most remarkable, at least on a formal and juridical level, concerns the Justinian *Digesto* on the right of association. It is common knowledge that before it came to its end the Roman Empire handed down the *Digesto*, a collection of juridical laws and regulations. Among these there is the heading XXII, (De Collegiis et corporibus), which specifically concerns the prohibition of unauthorised societies. On these grounds, the corporations which existed only occasionally during the Roman Empire, returned to favour after its fall and flourished until the birth of the Signories and the Monarchies. From the fourteenth to the eighteenth century, the corporations disappeared in Europe. Only those in the British Isles, where Roman Law was never accepted, were saved. This is the main reason why Freemasonry flourished in England at the beginning of the eighteenth century without having to claim its right of existence. In the European States, however, where it was rapidly spreading, the right of association was explicitly denied, on the very grounds of the *Digesto*. As a consequence, whoever saw danger in the masonic society had only to denounce it as a violation of the laws in force. Even in this case, in order to obtain guarantees for its own existence, Freemasonry had to engage in civil battle for the right of association.

The Civil States assumed different attitudes towards Freemasonry. On the one hand, there were those that defended constituted privileges, and opposed Freemasonry as a revolutionary danger. On the other were States which sharing the principles that were slowly transforming the old society, accepted the collaboration Freemasonry offered and consequently recognised its right to exist. The two attitudes were characteristic of the same State, at different stages in its development (a typical example can be seen in the history of Italy from 1870 to the present day). In the pages that follow, I will give as examples, cases taken from the history of Western civilisation.

England reflects the situation that characterises *par excellence* the absence of State condemnation against Freemasonry. As we have already indicated, this is partly due to the fact that the British Isles, being alien to the spread of Roman Law, did not impose any restraints or limits on the right of association. Therefore, the Freemasonry is not regarded as a secret society plotting against the powers of the State. What is secret in it is given by the initiatic foundation, and this secrecy therefore, does not disturb the rest of those in power. Secondly, members of the Royal Family and the aristocracy belong to Freemasonry. This also allows a direct control over the purposes of Freemasonry which, being acceted in its authentic sense, does not cause the State any anxiety. Indeed, these aims are partly the aims of the State as well, especially where cultural, educational and social problems are concerned. Consequently, Freemasonry is almost public.

Likewise in the United States of America. The model State of the colonists can only be, at least as regards its fundamental principles, that of the Motherland. But since the fathers of the American Revolution, from Washington to Franklin, had to reconstruct the State in conditions that were in some ways new and different with respect to England, they transferred the shared principles of Freemasonry to the Constitution of the United States. And so now the State, in realising Masonic ideals has no need for any sanctions against masonic societies. Furthermore, the role of Freemasonry in that country is perfectly understandable if we consider that seventeen Presidents of the United States were masons. In America, as in England, Freemasonry collaborates with the State to solve important and urgent problems of political and social life. Given these premises, masonic life in the United States is carried out for the most part in a public form. A great number of masons take part in the parades during festivities and solemn occasions, wearing their aprons. Each time the first stone of a new masonic Temple is laid, it is a solemn occasion for the whole town in which the highest authorities of the State take part. The traditional tie with the spirit of the Constitution is such that American Freemasonry does not only become a keeper of it, but it is also encouraged to take part in public activities of education and assistance. In fact, since it moves from the presupposition that concepts of the community already find expression in the school, it committed itself in favour of compulsory education, where each child, whatever its social class, creed or ethnic background must attend school. But it also constructed schools and universities. In the field of medical assistance, it collected funds for the building of hospitals and research institutes.

The situation changes radically when we move to European and non-European countries which have been subject to Roman Law. Freemasonry, in fact, is able to exist and develop only where enlightened governments do not oppose the affirmation of those principles that are slowly transforming modern society, and see in Freemasonry a valid ally. In all other cases, Freemasonry is persecuted or partially tolerated. This regularity has been confirmed in the history of European countries since the beginning of the eighteenth century until today. However, even if this historical investigation is significant, it lies outside the aim of this work. I will therefore give only a few examples.

I have already emphasised the important role Frederick II of Prussia played in favour of Freemasonry, when I examined the constitutional origins of the Ancient and Accepted Scottish Rite and showed that its present structure and organisation was due to the this sovereign's work. I would like to add here that it was not limited to an activity within Freemasonry, but it deeply influenced the framework of the State. In fact, when Frederick ascended the throne in 1740, he openly declared that he was a mason and consequently, issued laws which in every disposition, reflected tolerance: in particular, he suppressed torture and limited censorship. As a result, culture reached notable forms of expression too. After his death, Freemasonry was tolerated and then opposed until it was totally eliminated by Nazism.

Italy was no exception to the rule. From the unification up to the end of the First World War, Italian political orders were notably influenced by masonic principles and, in many aspects, the lay State and Freemasonry coincided. And so, Italian Freemasonry was not subjected to any condemnation or persecution from the State. However, the situation radically changed with the rise of Fascism. In fact, it was not long after the march on Rome that Freemasonry and Fascism came into conflict. The Great Council of Fascism, presided over by Mussolini, approved after lengthy discussion in the sitting of 13th February 1921, a resolution which read that 'Freemasonry pursues plans and uses methods that oppose those which inspire the activity of Fascism'. On 18th February 1923, the Board of the Grand Orient, with the Grand Master Domizio Torrigiani acting as chairman, deliberated in view of the new situation, that 'Fascist brothers are completely free to break all ties with Freemasonry', after which, many Fascist masons abandoned Freemasonry, while others, renouncing all the privileges that Fascism could offer them, turned their backs on Mussolini.

Meanwhile, towards the end of 1923, Fascist squads began to hit at some masonic Lodges; in Prato and Pistoia the Lodges 'G. Mazzini' and 'Ferruccio' were devastated; in Termoli the library of the Lodge 'E. Nathan' was destroyed; the Lodge of Monteleone was attacked by soldiers during a ceremony. After such devastations, the Grand Orient ordered that the brothers should choose between Freemasonry and Fascism. Acts of violence started up again: the Lodges of Genoa, Livorno, Pisa, Venice, Perugia, Bologna and Palermo were devastated and sacked; in Rome, the seat of the Grand Orient in the Giustiniani Palace was repeatedly attacked.

Tension increased. In the middle of December 1924, Torrigiani gave a speech in Milan in which he claimed that Fascism for Italy was a step backwards from a spiritual and moral point of view and that it reflected a return to criminal methods against the State. On January 10th 1925, the Ministery of Home Affairs proposed a new law in Parliament against secret societies which was in fact, it intended as a death blow to Freemasonry. The first article of this law established that all societies, corporations and institutions active in Italy were to hand in their act of foundation and their statute to the police, together with a list of their members and of those who had a position on the directive board. If the information given was false or incomplete the societies risked being be dissolved. Another article established that all employees of the State, Provinces and Town Councils as well as State dependent Institutes were forbidden to be members of secret societies or societies that, by means of an oath, were committed to a secret. Transgressors risked being dismissed. The law on secret societies was taken to Parliament to be discussed in May 1925. There is an interesting speech given by Mussolini in which he declared, 'My principle is this: To my friends, all my heart, to my enemies, all that is evil! Therefore, I will fight to the end against Freemasonry. This project shows the intimate coherence of my whole life . . . The law will show that Freemasonry has had its day and that in our century, it may not exist.'

After this law had been approved, many Lodges suspended their activities, while the Grand Orient continued to oppose Fascism.

Meanwhile, the climate of persecution against masons became more and more unbearable. When the Freemasonry was accused of being responsible for the fall of the lira in Florence, Brindisi and many other cities, masons were pulled out of their offices and brutally beaten, shops destroyed and Lodges wrecked. In particular, the Directorate of Fascism in Florence issued the following document in which violence was encouraged: 'From today forward, neither masons nor Freemasonry can remain even for an instant free from persecution. Masons, their belongings and their interests must be annihilated without mercy. They must be thrown out of public employment . . . with no exception. Good citizens must avoid the company of all masons. Under the weight of our strength they must be isolated as if they were lepers: we declare war on this society of cowards and we wish to do our duty by finally freeing Italy from these fierce enemies'. This declaration was posted overnight on the windows and shutters of all the shops belonging to masons. At last the result they wanted was obtained. For four days in Florence, it became legal to hunt down masons, many of whom were forced to leave the city, others were brutally beaten and forced to hand in their notice in public offices. Masons were literally massacred by an frenzied and ferocious crowd. When Mussolini ordered that this 'retaliation' should stop, eighteen had already died and fourty had been seriously injured.

Following these acts of violence, as a precautionary measure to protect masons from being exposed to such acts, the Grand Master of the Grand Orient declared that the works of all the Lodges in the national territory should stop. Since violence against Italian Freemasonry had placed Fascism in a negative light abroad, Mussolini realised he had to dispel this image and so agreed to be interviewed by an American journalist, K. H. Wiegand, to whom he maintained that 'in Germany, England and America, masons were a charitable and philanthropical fraternity. But in Italy, masons were a secret political organisation. What is more, and worse still, they completely depend on the Grand Orient of Paris. I hope that Italian masons will become like English and American masons, that is a fraternal and political society of mutual benefit'.

After the fall of Fascism, the democratic and republican institutions did not know how to (or did not want to) guarantee freedom of association. In fact, article 18 of the Italian Constitution says: '*Citizens have the right to associate freely,* without authorisation, for ends which are not prohibited to the individual by penal law. *Secret societies are probibited* as well as those that follow, even indirectly, political ends through organizations of a military nature'. This formulation is clearly ambiguous in that, while on the one hand, it *allows* citizens to associate freely, on the other it imposes a restriction on this freedom by *prohibiting* secret societies. Therefore not all societies are free. The democratic and republican State, at least as far as the secret was concerned, did not know how to (or want to) differentiate itself from the totalitarian State and insisted on seeing in the secret possible covers for plots and conspiracies. Since the debate in the Constituent Assembly on secret societies was implicitly directed at Freemasonry, the formulation of article 18 was again purposely misleading about the nature of masonic initiation. I intend to emphasise here that the initiation secret is an original and essential notion of masonic philosophical anthropology, without which Freemasonry, as an initiatic society, is no longer Freemasonry. At most, it becomes a society with philanthropical aims.

Supporters of the second clause of article 18 also intended to inflict another serious blow on Freemasonry when they refused to *define the criteria* for explaining the notion of a 'secret society'. These criteria would, at least, have guaranteed for Freemasonry the right not to be confused with other secret societies. On the other hand, leaving the notion of 'secret societies' undefined, the idea was to confer on the State the right of establishing, from time to time, what should be understood as a secret society. Endowed with this interpretative power, the democratic State could, for example, interpret the secret in the same way as the Fascist State, and thus, provoke the same persecutions in regard to masons. That this was not indeed a whim is evident from the recent decision of the State to authorise the confiscation of the lists of Italian masons, thus beginning, at least on a moral level, a witch hunt. There is clearly a lack of criteria for differentiating Freemasonry from other secret societies. Consequently, in order to guarantee its own existence, Freemasonry finds that one of its principal tasks is to renew its pledge to realise, in a democratic and republican society, an authentic and complete freedom of association.

Epilogue

Now that we have come to the end of our investigation, the reader will expect to find a summary of the thesis discussed in the previous nine chapters. I intend to carry out this task not by dwelling on the specific contents of each chapter, but rather by trying briefly to draw together the conclusions of a historical and theoretical nature that we have gradually reached and to place them in a unitary vision in the light of the underlying fundamental theme of the book, regarding the philosophical analysis of Freemasonry.

So now it is natural that the reader should ask: does a philosophy of Freemasonry exist, and in the case of a positive reply, which philosophy characterises masonic thinking? And again: is there a masonic anthropology and what relation can there be between it and anthropologies that are derived from other visions of the world? And finally: what are the documents in which this anthropology can be said to find its codification? What is binding about these writings? Is it worth looking at these documents again with a view to their being reformulated more consistently with respect to the present day and more in accordance with the expectations of future generations? I will try to give separate answers to these three orders of question.

Masonic thought does not express a philosophy, if by philosophy we mean a complete system including the totality of circles with which philosophical reflection is traditionally concerned. However it is upheld by a precise practical philosophy regarding man, his nature and his aims. This is why I have laid so much importance on masonic anthropology. The essential nucleus of masonic practical philosophy is in fact constituted by masonic anthropology. What do we mean by masonic anthropology? And before that, what do we mean by anthropology? We have already taken anthropology to mean a philosophical discourse on man telling us what his nature is, what sense his life has, what ideals his action derives significance from. In the course of its history, masonic thought itself has elaborated a discourse on man, emphasising and codifying some necessary characteristics, which, altogether make up the constituent elements of masonic anthropology and can be gathered together in the quintuple *Freedom, Tolerance, Brotherhood, Transcendence, Initiation Secret*. Of these, Freedom and Transcendence are the two fundamental notions around which the whole masonic anthropological system revolves. Given the importance of the argument, it is worthwhile taking it up again and elaborating upon it even in this concluding section.

The idea of freedom as Freemasonry understands it, presents a rather complex internal articulation, that makes it an essential requirement of the interior life of man and a foundation of his moral tension directed towards transcendence. According to masonic anthropology, man is free because he is allowed the possibility of deliberating on an objectively given order of values, which on the strength of this intentionability, reflects a determining potential component in the subjective order of values that he in fact follows in the responsible choice of his own actions. In other words, man is capable of making responsible choices, that ethically orientate his life, since his decisions are not the mere product of a pure judgement of utility associated with the determinism of his natural inclinations, but are a result of his capacity to follow a frame of objective values which, once understood, set off his ethical tension. This is why the notion of freedom would have little sense without the idea of transcendence next to it. The presence of a transcendent principle (expressed in the form of T.G.A.O.T.U.) has the precise function of guaranteeing the objectivity of an order of values from which the very idea of the betterment of man derives.

On the other hand, it is around the concept of transcendence that the debate has developed and led to various historical interpretations. Is T.G.A.O.T.U. an expression of the actual existence of a Supreme Being or simply the expression of a regulative principle in the process of the betterment of man? Our lengthy discussion on this subject (particularly in the chapter on the relationship between Freemasonry and religion), allows us to affirm that it is not essential for masonic anthropology (even if possible for each individual mason) that T.G.A.O.T.U. should be understood as a physically existing principle. Indeed, if the transcendent has the exclusive function of guaranteeing the objectivity of the intentionable values of man in his ethical choices, T.G.A.O.T.U. need not be understood as an ontologically given reality. He only needs to be understood as the regulative principle of the ethical order, an expression of a desire for transcendence which is at the root of man's moral tension. On the other hand, this does not exclude the fact that the *individual* mason may identify T.G.A.O.T.U. with the god of his religious faith, endowed with an inevitable ontological reality, the origin and end of all reality (and not only guarantor of the ethical dimension of man).

These are in brief the conclusions we reached in Chapter 6, where the more correct meaning to be given to transcendence in masonic thought was called non-exclusive regulativism. It follows that, in the idea of transcendence, there is some requisite, consisting in the regulative function of T.G.A.O.T.U. This regulative function however, does not exclude the fact that the individual mason may confer on T.G.A.O.T.U. a further sense in which he is identified with the god of the mason's own religious faith. On the other hand, this dimension of a further sense does not rival the image that Freemasonry as a society of men has of transcendence. And this is the root of the other two elements that make up masonic anthropology—tolerance and brotherhood.

As we have already said, tolerance does not consist in accepting everything and the opposite of everything, but in maintaining that, as far as the concept of the betterment of man is concerned, men of different faiths can find themselves in agreement provided they recognise on a minimal scale of values the essential values that for Freemasonry allow ethical betterment. Similar considerations can be made regarding the concept of brotherhood. Where T.G.A.O.T.U. is valued as the regulative principle all men are equal and consequently brothers on the road to perfection.

Naturally the burden of the initiatic secret hangs over masonic anthropology. Regarding the specific content of the rituals that Freemasonry practices with a view to putting man on the road to perfection, the secret gives a particular connotation to the masonic conception of man. In spite of its weight and importance, it does not alter the frame of reference within which non-exclusive regulativism defines the position of masonic anthropology in relation to the position inherent in other conceptions of the world. Masonic anthropology essentially centres on the ethical dimension of man and for this very reason, there is nothing to stop it from being enriched by the contributions of other anthropologies which centre on further dimensions of the human being. But such enrichment is not essential to masonic anthropology as such. If a mason is happy to conceive the transcendent as a regulative principle, he will recognise himself in a vision of man centred around his ethical dimension. But what about the one who, on the basis of his religious faith, sees man not only in his ethical but religious dimension as well? Is he likely to be denied access to Freemasonry because his anthropology is more complex than masonic anthropology? From the point of view of non-exclusive regulativism, this cannot be a sufficient condition for being barred. Only those positions of faith which are incompatible with the minimal frame of ethical values maintained by Freemasonry are incompatible with it. In short, we can say that masonic anthropology is a non-exclusive anthropology, a scheme of anthropology that can be accepted as a minimal anthropology, a matrix of anthropologies that are different yet converge in the same moral image of man.

The results we have reached on the structure of masonic anthropology lead us to some further conclusions on the compatibility between sharing masonic anthropology and accepting a religious faith. In the chapter on anthropology, we said that belonging to Freemasonry involved, among other things, acceptance of masonic anthropology in the connotation outlined above. This means in particular, that a mason can be neither an atheist nor share an integralist vision of masonic thinking. The first veto derives from the fact that a declaration of atheism cannot be compatible with the acceptance of a transcendence even in the ethical sense (implying the conception of T.G.A.O.T.U. as a regulative principle). The second is an expression of the fact that the principles of Freemasonry imply an intolerant attitude towards those who, belonging legitimately to Freemasonry, claim that the image of man as maintained by Freemasonry 'can be integrated' with the image, for example, of specific religious faiths. The second veto is thus a consequence of the principle of tolerance, itself a constituent element of masonic anthropology.

If a non-integralist vision of masonic thought is required of the mason, in conformity with the same constituent principles of masonic anthropology, the very non-integralist vision of one(s own religious belief is also a requirement the mason must satisfy when entering the Lodge, with the profession of his faith. Any form of integralism does not in fact allow one to recognise that there is a precise autonomy among the human dimensions, although they are linked together. A believer who assumes an integralist vision of his faith comes to believe that the ethical level is not autonomous with respect to the religious level but is absorbed by it. Consequently, since it makes no sense to him to speak of ethical betterment outside a religious context, he is necessarily led to think that those belonging to Freemasonry who do not share his same religious belief, are not actually capable of true ethical perfection. Therefore all forms of integralism are excluded from the anthropological conception of the mason. A mason who accepts masonic anthropology in its minimal form, cannot be integralist since he would conceive this anthropology exclusively, claiming that he was in his right to refuse participation in masonic work to associates professing some religious belief. In a specularly symmetric form, the mason-believer cannot be integralist because he would have to deny coherently the character of ethics to all masonic practice carried out by masons who hold no specific religious belief.

The reader who has given his attention not only to the demands of a theoretical order, but also to those inherent in the historical positions Freemasonry has held on various subjects might well now ask—Are the theoretical conclusions reached supported by the historical sources of Freemasonry? I will try to answer this question by dedicating these last few lines to the problem of interpreting the official documents of Freemasonry. On the basis of the ample historical documentation reviewed in this book, and in systematically reconstructing masonic anthropology, I have made more than enough references to the official sources of Freemasonry. On the other hand, a philological examination of the above might have allowed a sufficiently plausible degree of systematicity to be reached if certain interpretative criteria for the sources themselves had not been adopted. It is therefore, on these criteria that I propose to make some concluding remarks.

The sources of Freemasonry can be divided into three broad categories: the Landmarks, the Constitutions of Anderson and the Declarations of the Grand Lodges. Without any doubt, the Constitutions of Anderson are the sources of a general nature of greatest authority, both because they represent the first and only written codification of the constituent principles of masonic thought and organisation on a hierarchical scale and also because they are constantly referred to in the activities of the Lodges. Also of great importance are the Declarations of the Grand Lodges. Their significance is limited to certain areas and they do not set out to perform a general function equivalent to the Constitutions of Anderson, even if on some issues (the issue regarding the relationship between Freemasonry and religion for example), their meaning is clear-cut. Consequently, they cannot be omitted from a theoretical interpretation. Finally, the Landmarks are documents which contain the constituent principles shared by certain Grand Lodges. For this reason, however much they may be considered as drafts of statutes, they cannot be assimilated, either by their authority or intended purpose, into the general Constitutions of Anderson.

Furthermore the sources of masonic thought are all in some way dated, either because they represent—as in the case of Anderson's Constitutions—the creation of an order associated with a certain historical period, or because they can be attributed, like the Landmarks, to individual Grand Lodges, located in time and space; or lastly because the Declarations of the Grand Lodges were made in specific circumstances in which the Lodges were asked to give their opinion on specific issues. In the task of historical reconstruction we must however, take all these elements into account globally and try to give each of the sources its correct weight in relation to its authority, its purpose and to its historical context. In this sense, the Constitutions of Anderson and the Declarations of the Grand Lodges are given a privileged place. As far as the Landmarks are concerned, they seem to be important more for their characteristic structure than for their content. They represent the codification of the convictions—including religious convictions—of those belonging to certain Grand Lodges. If it is true that there is no clear distinction in them between the masonic and religious spheres—for example, their not conforming to the prohibition of religious discussion in the Lodge—it is just as true that they show that masons of certain Grand Lodges found themselves historically or culturally at one with a specific religious faith, without feeling obliged to deny their overriding masonic identity. From this point of view, the Landmarks can be interpreted as giving historical support to my theory of non-exclusive regulativism.

To conclude, I believe I can say that in spite of the multiplicity of sources and the difficulties of interpreting them, a secure and stable unitary thought can be identified. The aim of this book has been to make a preliminary contribution to this interpretation and to the rational ordering of masonic thought. The need for this task of recognition and theoretical reconstruction is particularly urgent in an historical period such as ours, in which alongside the desire to return to the origins of masonic thought, there is also felt a need to give it a precise outline for the benefit of present and future generations, lest it be confused with others that have nothing to do with the masonic ideal.

Bibliography

ABAFI, L., *Geschichte der Freimaurerei in Osterreich-Ungarn*, Budapest, Selbstverl., 1890-1899, 5 vols.

ADLER, M.J., *The Idea of Freedom*, New York, 1958-1961, 2 vols.

ALDRIDGE, A.O., "Shaftesbury and the Deist Manifesto", in *Transactions of the American Philosophical Society*, new ser., Vol 41, Part (1951), pp.297-385.

ANDERSON, J., *The Old Constitutions Belonging to the Ancient and Honourable Society of Free and Accepted Masons of England and Ireland*, edited by J. Cox, London, Spencer, 1871.

ANDERSON, J., *Constitutions of the Freemasons of the Premier Grand Lodge of England, 1815-1896*, edited by W. Hughan, London, Kenning, 1899.

BODIN, J., *Six Livres de la République*, 1576.

BOLLER, P.F.,Jr, *George Washington and the Religion*, Dallas, Texas, 1963.

BORD, G., *La Franc-Maçonnerie en France, des Origines á 1815*, Paris, Nouvelle Librairie Nationale, 1909.

BURTON, R., *The Anatomy of Melancholy*, 1621.

BURY, J.B., *A History of Freedom of Thought*, New York, 1913.

CALVERT, A., *The Grand Lodge of England, 1717-1917*, London, Jenkins, 1917.

CHEVALLIER, P., *Histoire de la Franc-Maçonnerie Française*, Paris, Fayard, 1974-1975, 3 vols.

CLAUSEN, H.C., *Clausen's Commentaries on Morals and Dogma*, San Diego, California, 2nd ed, Neyenesch Printers, 1976.

CLAUSEN, H.C., *Messages for a Mission*, San Diego, California, Neyenesch Printers, 1977.

CLAUSEN, H.C., *Authentics of a Fundamental Law for Scottish Rite Freemasonry*, San Diego, Neyenesch Printers, 1979.

CLAUSEN, H.C., *Practice and Procedure for the Scottish Rite*, San Diego, Neyenesch Printers, 1981.

COLLINS, A., *A Discourse of Freethinking*, 1713.

CORDIER, A., *Histoire de l'Ordre Maçonnique en Belgique*, Mons, H. Chevallier, 1854.

CORETH, E., *Was ist der Mensch? Grundzuge einer philosophischen Anthropologie*, Innsbruck, Tyrolia Verlag, 1976.

DI BERNARDO, G., *Le regole dell'azione sociale*, Milano, il Saggiatore, 1983.

DRYDEN, J., *Religio Laici*, 1682.

DYER, C., *Symbolism in Craft Freemasonry*, London, Lewis Masonic, 1988.

ESPOSITO, R.F., *Pio IX La Chiesa in conflitto col mondo*, Roma, Edizioni Paoline, 1979.

FAY, B., *Franklin the Apostle of Modern Times*, Boston, Little Brown, 1929.

FERRER BENIMELI, J. and CAPRILE, G., *Chiesa e Massoneria: ieri, oggi, domani*, Roma, Edizioni Paoline, 1979.

FICHTE, J.G., *Philosophie der Maurerei*, neu herausgegeben und eingeleitet von Wilhelm Flitner, Leipzig, Meiner, 1923.

GAMBERINI, G., *Attualità della Massoneria. Gli operai sono contenti?*, Ravenna, Longo, 1978.

GOULD, R.F., *The History of Freemasonry*, London, Jack, 1884-1887, 6 vols.

HANFLIN, O., *Logical Positivism*, Oxford, Basil Blackwell, 1981.

HEFELBOWER, S.G., *The Relation of John Locke to English Deism*, Chicago, 1918.

HERBERT OF CHERBURY, E., *De Veritate*, 1624.

HEWITT, A.R., *The Grand Lodge of England; History of the First 100 Years*, Ars Quatuor Coronatorum, vol.80, 1967.

HORTON, J. and MENDUS, S. (eds), *Aspects of Toleration*, London, Methuen, 1985.

HUGHAN, W.J., *Origin of the English Rite of Freemasonry*, edited by J.T.Thorp, Leicester, 1909.

JACKSON, A.C.F., *ROSE CROIX: A History of the Ancient and Accepted Rite for England and Wales*, London, Lewis Masonic, 1988.

JACOBS, B., *Scandinavian Freemasonry*, Ars Quatuor Coronatorum, vol.72, 1960.

JONES, B.E., *Freemasons' Guide and Compendium*, London, Harrap, 1950.

JORDAN, W.K., *Development of Religious Toleration in England*, Cambridge, Mass., 1932-1940, 4 vols.

JOUAUST, *Histoire du Grand Orient de France*, Paris, Teissier, 1865.

KANT, I., *Critique of Practical Reason*, 1788.

KANT, I., *Religion within the Limits of Reason Alone*, 1792-1794.

LENNHOF, E., *The Freemasons*, London, Methuen; new edition, London, Lewis, 1978.

LESSING, G.E., *Nathan the Wise*, 1779.

LIGOU, D., *La Franc-Maçonnerie*, Paris, Presses Universitaires de France, 1977.

MORAIS, H.M., *Deism in Eighteenth Century America*, New York, 1934.

Memorials of the Masonic Union of 1813, edited by W.J. Hughan, Leicester, Johnson, Wykes and Paine, 1913.

MILL, J.S., *On Liberty*, London, 1859; Penguin edition, Himmelfarb (ed.),Harmondsworth, 1974.

MOLA, A.A., *Storia della Massoneria italiana dall'Unità alla Repubblica*, Milano, Bompiani, 1976.

MOLINARI, F., *La Massoneria*, Brescia, Queriniana, 1981.

NAUDON, P., *La Franc-Maçonnerie*, Paris, Presses Universitaires de France, 1981.

NAUDON, P., *Histoire genérale de la Franc-Maçonnerie*, Office du Livre, Fribourg (Suisse), 1981.

OGILVIE, E. and THOMPSON, H.A., *Freemasons' Royal Arch Guide*, London, Lewis Masonic, 1988.

PIKE, A., *Morals and Dogma*, Charleston, 1871.

READ, J., *Prelude to Chemistry*, London, 1936.

ROBERTSON, J.M., *A Short History of Freethought Ancient and Modern*, London, 1915, 2 vols.

RUSSELL, B., "Freedom and Government", in R.N. Anshen (ed), *Freedom: Its Meaning*, New York, 1940.

RUSSELL, B., *Why I Am Not a Christian and Other Essays on Religion and Related Subjects*, P. Edwards (ed), London, 1957.

SPINOZA, B., de, *Tractatus Theologico-Politicus*, 1670, in *The Chief Works of Spinoza*, New York, 1955.

TAYLOR, S., *The Alchemists*, London, 1952.

Tempio Scozzese, series of the Ancient and Accepted Scottish Rite, Roma, 1984-1985, 6 vols.

The Regius Poem, Masonic Book Club, Bloomington, I11., 1970.

TINDAL, M., *Christianity as Old as the Creation, or, the Gospel A Republication of the Religion of Nature*, 1730.

TOLAND, J., *Christianity Not Mysterious*, 1696.

TORREY, N.L., *Voltaire and the English Deists*, New Haven, 193O.

VIRET, P., *Instruction chrétienne*, Geneva, 1564.

VOLTAIRE, *Trait sur la tolerance*, 1763.

WELLS, R.A., *Royal Arch Matters*, London, Lewis Masonic, 1984.

WELLS, R.A., *Some Royal Arch Termes Examined*, London, Lewis Masonic, 1988.

WELLS, R.A., *The Rise and Development of Organised Freemasonry*, London, Lewis Masonic, 1988.

WILMSHURST, W.L., *The Meaning of Masonry*, New York, Bell Publishing Company, Distributed by Crown Publishers, 1980.

Index